Prayers of Sherkin
and
Boss Grady's Boys

Prayers of Sherkin
'The story is of a dwindling group on Sherkin Island, brought there two generations earlier by Matt Purdy, an awkward artisan from the black city of Manchester, to abide until the dawn of the new Jerusalem . . . The play is like a gentle requiem for a dead community, as it conjures visions of a world that might have been and a people fixed too rigidly in their own love and lore.'
(David Nowlan, *Irish Times*)

'In beautiful and languid language, it captures those moments of change in a way that no historian could, the moment at which ideology and cherished doctrine are discarded for the sake of survival . . . This is a haunting and evocative play and it lingers with you long after the curtain goes down.' (Brian Brennan, *Sunday Independent*)

Boss Grady's Boys
'Barry's writing has a subtlety which puts Boss Grady's Boys into a different league from the vast majority of plays that have been written about rural Ireland since Synge.' (*Sunday Press*)

'Boss Grady's Boys has an emotional intensity, a theatrical fluidity and a sense of humanity that are rare and very special. Barry keeps a miraculous balance between ironic absurdity and unrestrained yearning, between Mick and Josey's comic awareness of their own situation and the love and pity which underlie that awareness.'
(Fintan O'Toole, *Sunday Tribune*)

Sebastian Barry was born in Dublin in 1955 where he still lives. He was elected to Aosdana in 1989 and was Ansbacher Writer-in-Residence at the Abbey Theatre, Dublin in 1990. His plays include **The Pentagonal Dream** (Damer Theatre, Dublin, 1986); **Boss Grady's Boys** (Abbey Theatre, Peacock stage, Dublin, 1988) which won the first BBC/Stewart Parker Award and **Prayers of Sherkin** (Abbey Theatre, Peacock stage, Dublin, 1990). He has also published several works of both poetry and fiction.

Methuen New Theatrescripts series offers frontline intelligence of the most original and exciting work from the fringe:

Prayers of Sherkin
Boss Grady's Boys

Two plays by
Sebastian Barry

Methuen Drama

A Methuen New Theatrescript

This collection first published in Great Britain in 1991 by Methuen
Drama, Michelin House, 81 Fulham Road, London SW3 6RB and
distributed in the United States of America by HEB Inc., 361
Hanover Street, Portsmouth, New Hampshire NH 03801 3959.

Boss Grady's Boys first published in 1989 by the Raven Arts Press,
Dublin, Ireland.

ISBN 0-413-65660-8

A CIP catalogue record for this book is available
from the British Library.

The front cover shows Alison Deegan as Fanny from **Prayers of
Sherkin**. Photograph copyright © Fergus Bourke, 1990.

Printed and bound in Great Britain
by Cox & Wyman Ltd, Cardiff Road, Reading

Introduction

Prayers of Sherkin

In 1985 I landed back in Ireland after a few years of restlessness in Europe. I was at home, homesick for abroad. I knew nobody in Dublin, and there was a certain distance between my family and myself. It wasn't good, I thought, something had to be done.

As usual none of my own efforts came to much, but the God of Dublin arranged that I would meet someone who would show me how to love the city, how to work in it, how to be a Dubliner. This was the great luck, and that person also renovated the house of my work, and is responsible I should think for the better bits of this play.

But all Dubliners are the children of country people, or grandchildren, or great-grandchildren. Since I was now to be an Irishman, it seemed I would have to make myself up as I went. I was casting about, looking for fragments of information with a bit of glitter to them, clues to the dark paintings in the dark caves. But it was by no real effort of mine that I heard the name of Fanny Hawke. Just accident. As soon as she lodged, with her few surviving facts, the very shadow of her true life, a piece of old thread, she set up house good and proper. For a few years I thought about her, wrote a poem for her, mulled over her courage and the silence surrounding her some forty years after her death. For in those days to be a lower Protestant was one thing, but to pass from this state into the cold Catholic world . . .

Fanny Hawke, Fanny Hawke . . . Her name will always be a kind of secular prayer for me. And yet I know that I really made her up from one or two old remarks about her; I made her up; I think I made her up.

One evening after the show a woman of about sixty stood up in the row in front of me, turned about, held my arm, and said: 'Fanny Hawke was my grandmother and she was just like that. She spoke like that. There was a man in America that wanted her to marry him, but she told us that "she had no true wish to go to him". She was just like that, gentle, and her son, my father, was gentle like that too.'

Home at last.

Boss Grady's Boys

A play that paid the rent for the first time in a writing career of
ten years or so. Gratitude, gratitude . . . Ideal director, ideal
light, ideal cast. The two actors in the main roles, Eamon Kelly
and Jim Norton, making the writer more content than a writer
has a right to be.

I wrote **Boss Grady's Boys** to repay a human debt to a pair
of real brothers in a real corner of Cork, where I had lived for a
while in 1982. These were two magnificent kindly men who were
quick to talk to me on the track between our houses, and as
quick to keep away if they thought that was wiser. One night the
real Mick carried up a sack of swedes and turnips as a present.
Another evening I spotted him in a special part of the housefield,
standing alone and silent, watching the sun going, his hat on his
head. Perhaps when I went they forgot me. I was just a bit of
passing weather. But while I was there they looked out for me,
they kept a weather eye out, they included me in their cares.
Oddly enough, I was never actually inside their house.

A couple of years later there was a spate of attacks on old
couples living alone in the countryside in Ireland. Someone was
going around in vans and talking their way into the lives of such
people, getting their confidence, and robbing them. In a district
of Mayo I knew well, I learned of two old brothers who had
suffered this. One of them had been killed, the other ended up in
the county home.

Naturally, though I knew they were strong and secure in their
ways, I thought of my two friends in Cork. I hoped if I wrote a
play about such a life it would have some value, if only as a
talisman against evil, for them.

After Eamon Kelly read the play and said he could do it, it
transpired that he had grown up not too many fields away from
the very place the play was trying to illustrate. He knew that
world better than a local rook. Casting like that is hard to
arrange.

By the time we were finished, I might have drawn a strange
demographic map of Ireland consisting of older brothers living
alone together, we gathered news of so many such lives.

What puzzled me for a long time was the scene with the

toothbrush. I didn't really know why there was a toothbrush in Mick's jacket pocket. Then one summer night I walked up to the house in Mayo where the other brothers had had their day of terror. Their fields had been scraped already by a bulldozer, the interior of their house was dark and poor and scattered with oddments. Outside the back door someone had tossed a box of this and that, an old pill-bottle, a comb; and, still in its plastic wrapper, proud and pristine, an excellent toothbrush.

Sebastian Barry
March 1991

Prayers of Sherkin

For Barney, Maureen, Henry and Barbara,
the four friends.

Prayers of Sherkin was first performed at the Abbey Theatre (Peacock stage), Dublin, on 20 November 1990 with the followng cast:

Fanny	Alison Deegan
John	Alan Barry
Hannah	Doreen Hepburn
Sarah	Joan O'Hara
Jesse	Phelim Drew
Mr Moore	Eamon Kelly
Eoghan	Owen Roe
Patrick	Brendan Gleeson
Meg	Ruth McCabe
Stephen	Wesley Murphy
Singer	Gina Moxley
Matt Purdy	Donal O'Kelly

Directed by Caroline FitzGerald
Designed by Bronwen Casson
Lighting by Tony Wakefield
Music by Shaun Davey

Characters

Fanny Hawke, *thirty, plain.*
John Hawke, *her father, sixties.*
Hannah Hawke, *her aunt,* **John**'s *sister, bowed back.*
Sarah Purdy, *sister of* **Fanny**'s *mother. Arc of white hair.*
Jesse Hawke, **Fanny**'s *brother, thin.*

Mr Moore, *the ferryman, fit, seventies.*
Eoghan O'Drisceoil, *fisherman, from Cape Clear.*

Patrick Kirwin, *lithographer, forty.*
Meg Pearse, *shopkeeper, handsome.*
Stephen Pearse, *her husband, considerably older.*
Singer, *impoverished woman, twenty.*

Matt Purdy, *the founder of the sect, in the form of an angel.*

Setting: Sherkin Island and Baltimore, County Cork. 1890s.

Act One

Curtain. A shadowy stage, except for **John**'s *workshop. Dusty late sunlight through a high window. Ten candles hanging from their rack, partly formed by ladling.* **Jesse** *with a simple basin. The broom in its place on pegs. They wear plain trim workclothes with natural-coloured aprons. Their accent is Sherkin with a tint of Manchester.*

Jesse Will you clean off your own hands now?

John (*looking at light*) I think I must. (*At candles.*) Another while of care for these characters. (*Washing his hands.*) But not this day, Jesse. Did you douse the wax-fire?

Jesse I did douse it, softly, Father.

John Give it another douse with this water now.

Jesse *goes off. He casts the water into a small stove. It hisses and steams.* **John** *takes the long-footed brush and begins to sweep in a careful style. Dust stirs.*

Does it build again?

No answer. **Jesse** *has headed home.* **John** *sweeps.*

A chandler must know his dirt. It is to be kept out of the yellow candles. And much the same caution for a baker. It is to be kept out of the bakery of his life. (*Light failing.*)

Outside. The whitethorn with its September berries. A low fresh moon in a late daylight sky. **Jesse** *comes on alone, without apron, a few candles in his hand. He sits in under whitethorn as is his practice. Scratches at the roots vaguely. Hugs his knees. The moon freshening, the face and form of* **Matt Purdy** *in the moon's gentle light. He is small and ordinary, he*

*wears the 1790s clothes of an artisan from Manchester, and his accent is
the same, strong and sincere.* **Jesse** *does not see him.*

Matt Purdy We embarked from the dark port of England and
sailed to Cork in the whitest ship. There were storms in the
purple sea and there were fruitful fishes, and the three families
clung to the rails and found their haven. We followed the
message that came to me in the dark of Manchester, under the
chimneys and the black moon, the bright words ran over the
rainy roofs and over the tumultuous graveyards of that city and
over the factories where the children sweated and over the heads
of the government officers and the policemen marching in the
squares and the purple soldiers. And I, Matt Purdy, had my
vision that was like unto the vision of John of Patmos, and it
came to me in my dreams to go to Ireland for to find an island
where we could abide. And we sailed out of the city of suffering
to Cork, and found out this little island of Sherkin where we
could wait for the city of light. Remember Thou the faith of the
Purdys, the Smiths, and the Hawkes.

Distantly off, **Fanny** *is calling* **Jesse**'s *name from the house. He scuffs
away out from under the tree, only the moon in place of* **Matt Purdy.**

The darkening main room of the **Hawke** *house. Very plain and
Quakerish, wooden, items on pegs. Two square windows, an unlit wood-
stove, a bench and two high-backed wooden chairs, one still hung on its
pegs. The other, brought over to the door,* **Fanny** *sits on, looking out. The
light from outside moves through like water. She wears the entirely
unadorned skirt and bodice of a Quakerlike sect of the 1890s, and an
evening headcloth. She is watching for* **Jesse** *and her father. The table is
set for five, with very simple bowls, white.* **Sarah** *comes in from kitchen
with a lit taper, worriedly guarding it, lights the five candles in the room.*
Fanny's *face brightens, she sits back a little, she sees someone coming.*
Hannah *comes in from the kitchen more abruptly, carrying a bowl of
steaming food.* **John** *steps in with* **Jesse** *on his heels.*

John Here is the nest of birds.

Fanny *gets up and kisses him, he rubs the kiss.*

If I had no kiss I might never come home.

Hannah (*looking at her work*) What a good plain table now.

They sit in their places, **John** *with* **Hannah** *and* **Sarah** *on the bench,* **Fanny** *and* **Jesse** *each side of them. They listen intently to* **John**.

John If you do please, Lord, this is our night prayer. We do ask you for the peace of this family. We do ask you for the silence and the storm of Sherkin. Once there were three families, Lord, that Matt Purdy led from Manchester. There were black chimneys there and the rotted streets, and they came for to wait for the new city. Lord, we do abide, even unto this third generation. There are no others. Lord, you have taken my wife Charity. Bring in your own time a plain husband from Manchester for this our daughter Fanny, and a plain wife for Jesse. Lord, we are not lonely but we are few. Send us your help. Lord, we pray that you have not forgotten us, your five remaining. Send us increase. May you not leave one of us alone here since all around are the darknesses of the Catholics and the strangenesses of the higher Protestants.

Sarah, *despite herself, sneaks out a hand to judge the warmth of the bowl.* **Hannah** *checks her.*

Lord, we trust in your promise to the poor and the revelation of your servant, John of Patmos, the blessed islander. Since he has shown that for us surely the New Jerusalem is by. Keep us ready for to be the tribe you mention, and let there be others still in Manchester though we have heard nothing of them for many a year. Lord, thank you for the prosperity of the candle manufactory and the ease of this plain house. Oh Lord, we do abide.

All We do abide.

They set to in silence. **Fanny** *looks back out through a window.*

Fanny The evening star, Jesse.

A simple music. The night deepens around them, the candlelight brighter. **Jesse** *takes a last careless spoon of food. He starts to choke.*

Hannah Oh, Jesse, you are too idle with food.

She pats his back.

Sarah Oh, Hannah, save his life.

Hannah I am saving his life now.

Jesse *better.*

Fanny His poor throat is crooked.

John He put it the wrong way. Bless you, child.

Hannah Now, Sarah, will we cross tomorrow to the yard? I have heaps of honeysuckle for the graves.

Sarah We could wait another week. I would have some selling butter then, in a week. I could hardly manage a batch tonight and tomorrow, dear.

Hannah I was thinking of the honeysuckle. I have never seen such good blooms. They would look well on the beds, now, would they not, Sarah?

John Moore would row you anyway, with or without butter.

Hannah Baltimore has butter enough without yours. (*After a bit.*) Though it is good butter. The best.

Sarah I do not like to cross without purpose.

Hannah Flowers is purpose enough.

Fanny And we would love to come, me and Jesse.

John (*to* **Sarah**) Now.

Sarah Well. The wicked thing is I love to cross. I dream of crossing. I am too attached to the town. I dream about that material in Pearse's. Wicked.

John Who is to mind a dream?

Sarah There is a ribbon-box too, Lord forgive me.

John Mr Moore will row you. I will give him a hand of candles as usual and he will row the lot of you and an angel to boot.

Sarah (*simply*) Matt Purdy saw five angels on the bridge crossing the great river. He saw them walking among the crowd of mortals, plain bright people with feathered wings.

John (*as a fact*) I never did see one. (*Rising, gathering bowls.*) Now, let us please the pig. You do not mind if I cast the remnant to the pig?

A little delay as **Hannah** *realises he is talking to her.*

Hannah He will be very cross if you do not.

They laugh. **John** *and* **Jesse** *go out with everything. The remaining three listen.*

Fanny He is serenading. I can hear him.

Hannah As near to a person as makes no odds, a pig.

John *and* **Jesse** *returning in good spirits.*

John A very fierce companionable pig.

Jesse The skeleton of a pig is similar to a man's.

John There is an observation. That boy has things in his head that only an angel would think of.

Hannah (*vaguely*) Oh, angels.

A simple music. **Sarah** *and* **Hannah** *alone.* **Hannah** *shakes out the white bedspread they are working on, some tiny sand-flowers already embroidered on it.* **Sarah** *brings to the table two more of the candles. The light is more theirs. She slips in under the cloth, the two of them begin to sew, together on the bench.*

Hannah Some peace now.

She winds her thread around thumb and forefinger on each hand with a quick practised movement, and snaps it.

At least the storm is not blowing again.

Sarah Or Fanny and Jesse could not have gone out.

Hannah It rattled the island. The lanes this morning were full of green branches.

Sarah Think of it far out at sea now, with all its froth and turmoil in the waves. Pleasant enough.

Hannah You would not say that if you were a sailor, like Mr Moore was once, or indeed a mere fish. I saw no big fish beached on the sand this morning this time. I did not see a blessed soul, only a man bringing his cart down, for weed.

Sarah Did you know him?

Hannah I think it was the hotel-keeper's cart. He has a little field of potatoes behind him. He would want the weed for that.

Sarah He has rights there to weed.

Hannah No doubt.

Sarah How many ships that were set for America, and foundered by Sherkin, no man knows.

Hannah I do believe you.

John *comes in from kitchen, peaceful with his book.* **Hannah** *and* **Sarah** *give him a smile. He takes down a chair and sits under a dark window.*

John May it not rain on the children.

Hannah Amen.

He settles, starts to read, almost immediately begins to daydream instead, flicking the clasp of the book.

(*The cloth is caught under something.*) Can you lift it from under your foot?

Sarah (*looking down*) It is not under any of my feet.

Hannah Ah, it is my own.

John Tell me, Hannah, what would be the best flowers to grow for bees?

Hannah Oh? Oh?

John There is no reason why we could not keep bees, I was thinking. It would save me buying in the wax from our little nuns. There were be no nuns' fees. There would be a great use in that. And I think it would give me a great pleasure, tending the bees. I understand there is a particular outfit for them, with a veil indeed. Something like a swordsman's outfit.

Hannah *smiles.*

Hannah Now, I imagine it would be the flowers with the best pollen.

Looks to **John** *for confirmation. He thinks, nods.*

Flowers with the best blooms. I imagine honeysuckle itself is a bee-attracting plant. I would be happy to grow more honeysuckle.

John Naturally, I could make the little houses myself. Jesse could do the designs. If I sent for a handbook, I think he might find it easy enough.

Sarah I cannot see it being too difficult for Jesse.

Hannah Mrs Pearse discussed a new flower with me, called the rhododendron. But I often saw bees on the gooseberries when they are flowering. Do you know, John, I feel the winds might be a bit rascally for bees here.

John (*accepting this*) Of course, we light the town already. A seaboard town. It is very good to stand on the pier and look over at Baltimore in the night and see the lights.

Sarah It is a great thing to light a town, I think.

John (*pleased*) The other day, when I was over in Baltimore, I

had a most pleasant talk with Mr Pearse. How likeable I find
him. He said there were never such candles in the world before
the Hawkes, the Purdys and the Smiths came to Sherkin. And
you know (*Laughing*.), he said his grandfather used to say that.

Hannah They are both very likeable, him and his wife.

John They are.

Sarah He is your special friend. And why not? You have every
right to be loved by any friend.

John You know, Sarah, it is often said that the heron is the
messenger. Sometimes you tell me a thing, and it has the force of
the message the heron holds for the privileged stranger.

A short gap.

Do you remember, Hannah, when you heaped Moore's boat
with honeysuckle, when we were bringing Charity over to the
yard? It is an egregious plant. It is something for the donning of
a corpse. Charity lying there. It was a kindness of Mr Moore's,
to carry her so in state. Hah, he is a man of excellence, Michael
Moore. Of the Catholic men on this island he is the paradigm.
There is always something to learn from Mr Moore. He has been
to very many places, in contrast to ourselves. There is a man
that can sing the song of Valparaiso and he knows he has been
there. He can see the streets of Valparaiso in his old head when
he sings his song. It is not just a name. He carried Charity over
to the yard heaped in honeysuckle. He rowed I think with a
special pride.

Sarah Well, now.

John (*almost to himself*) Of course, Moore has a hearth, and has
his hearth-lore. But we make do with our English stove.

The women shake out the cloth.

A sky of stars. The high moon. **Jesse** *and* **Fanny**.

Fanny Do you not feel that this island is moored only lightly to
the sea-bed, and might be off for the Americas at any moment?
Jesse?

Jesse *surveying the heavens.*

The pig would come with us, and never know, but that the
weather might change, and he would freckle. We would line up
with the Bahaman Islands and no one notice us, though I would
be sad to lose Clear Island out there with its people and
wandering lights. Oh, Jesse, we are not from here and I have
such a sense of home. I am always thankful that the holy couples
came here. They might have ended anywhere. I think it is the
site of our New Jerusalem, which is to come from the heavens,
right down from those stars.

Jesse *looks at her.*

You need not frown at me, I know you are not watching just
tonight for any holy city. (*To herself.*) It would frighten a lion
such a thought. (*To* **Jesse**.) You are careful of the stars for their
own sake. A technical brother, dear. And, Jesse, you are a
brother to excite something in my own head. There is a little
stage there, and the dancers appear. Lord, Jess, they are can-can
dancers like in the posters, and they are not speaking English.
Your stars set off the dancers, and they are lovely big women
with mad dresses, and whup, when they all kick their legs up,
may you have mercy, but they are wearing nothing beneath.

Jesse (*not heeding her*) But all very tussocky grass for a scientist to
lean his paper on.

Draws a pencil stub and a scrap of paper from a pocket. **Fanny** *lies on
the ground, stomach down.*

Fanny You can make me your table, Jesse.

Jesse *looks up at the stars again, and starts to mark their positions.*

The grass has a lovely smell. It smells of tiny flowers.

Jesse The stars are as small as flowers to us. That is because of their great distance from our concerns.

Fanny (*turning onto an elbow*) Is that why you care to draw them?

Jesse No, this is science, Fanny. It is to see their relative positions. Ursa Major, Ursa Minor. The names are best given in Latin.

Fanny Oh, do not give any more of them in Latin. (*Getting up.*) Do you see, Jesse, how the beacon on Cape Clear, and our own house there, like a star fallen to the fields, and your own evening star, mark such a big triangle in the sky?

Jesse Ursa Major, Ursa Minor.

Fanny I think we had better not stay here longer. I can feel the breath of the grass rising into me. We will be sitting at home creaking like creels with damp.

Jesse I have the work now. (*Stuffing the paper in his pocket.*) August is a month of wonders. Any man like me lives for August and its moon. But I do not scorn September, between storms.

The candles bring back the room again. **Hannah** *and* **Sarah** *have cleared away their work.* **John** *hangs up his chair and waits by the open door.*

Hannah We will go over to Baltimore tomorrow, John, me and Sarah and the children, to put honeysuckle on the families' graves, and to get whatever scientific purchases for Jesse as can be found in a little place like Pearse's.

Sarah (*taking a candle for bed*) Oh, my dear, Pearse's. A dangerous spot for an old lady like myself.

Hannah We might look over a few linens. (*To* **John**.) A few sober-dyed linens.

John *nods, peacefully.* **Fanny** *and* **Jesse** *appear out of the dark.*

John Oh. Why, you both smell of rain.

Sarah (*going out with her candle into kitchen*) In Pearse's tomorrow I will pass by the ribbons. I will not put my hand in the ribbon-box.

John (*taking a candle, showing book to* **John**) I did not see much of this.

Fanny *smiles, kisses him, kisses* **Jesse**. **Hannah** *is preparing the bench as a bed for* **Fanny**. **John** *puts his hand on* **Jesse**'*s shoulder and leads him over to the kitchen door.*

Hannah (*to* **John**) I have a jug of milk in the drip-press for your morning.

John (*smiling, looking down at* **Jesse** *as he says it*) That will suit me.

They go out.

Hannah This is a fresh bed, dear.

Fanny (*starting to take off her clothes*) It is very inviting.

Hannah (*taking up a candle from a window, seeing that there are also two more*) How are there three candles left?

She sets the candle with the other one on the table.

Fanny (*working at the buttons on her underclothes*) Jesse took no candle for his book. He must be very sleepy.

Hannah *holds a big nightdress for* **Fanny**, *standing in front of her.* **Fanny** *takes off the last of her things and over her head goes the nightdress.*

Hannah There, now.

Fanny *into bed.* **Hannah** *draws the clothes up over her, covering her arms.*

When you were little I used to sing to you now, did I not? If I was let. I have no voice and Charity was always jealous for your rest. And quite right.

Hannah *leans over* **Fanny**, *taking the pins out of the headcloth.* **Fanny** *sneaks her arms out and puts them around* **Hannah**'s *neck.* **Fanny** *seems both upset and happy.* **Hannah** *hugs her.*

Hannah Well. What is that story about? Now.

She disentangles herself and puts the headcloth with the other clothes, pats them.

Now. Put in your arms.

Fanny Do I look like her at all?

Hannah In this light, you could be her. Put in your arms.

Fanny Oh. (*Does so.*)

Hannah (*snuffs a candle, takes her own up*) I am glad there is no storm tonight. You will be asleep before I reach my own bed. Sleep well, child. God bless you.

Fanny And you, Aunty.

Hannah *goes off. A thickening of moonlight. The moon is big above the roof.* **Fanny** *takes her arms out again. Thinking. Stirs herself. Her prayer.*

The hour for a mother to come and kiss her child asleep. An hour darkened and sunken. Mine own hour that I cannot fear because of Jesse's concerns. There is a father asleep in his goose bed, there are two aunts in the same wooden room where they often slept as girls. There is a brother in his niche under the wooden stairs. There is a sleep over the islands. Cape Clear is low and dark on its own piece of dark sea, the lost glass lobster-floats bang in the deep sea-ravines, the dogs of the sea bark at each other on the bleak slabs. Peace to the Ganges, my God, the Amazon and the Shannon. Peace to the darting fishes and the crushed fishes of the very deep. Peace, my deepest Lord, to the great fold of shadow that the earth must draw around her in the night.

She sleeps. A simple music. The moon sets quicker than it could in real time. Light clears the ragged sky. A foot of sunlight creeps in over the windowsill. Enter **John**, *from kitchen, freshly shaved, clean, eager, simple, spick and span in his workclothes.*

John (*putting on his hat*) As long as there is dark there must be candles.

Fanny *wakes abruptly.*

Fanny Drowning!

John Drowning?

Fanny I was fighting in a waterfall of the Orinoco.

John Oh. Very good.

Sarah *comes in, already dressed for the town.*

Goodbye, Sarah.

Sarah Oh, goodbye, John. Do you have your cheese?

John *pats a pocket. He goes out.*

(*To herself.*) What a morning for creation. Fanny, go up to Hannah for your town dress. What a morning.

Fanny What a tremendous relief. You are dressed already?

Sarah What do you say, child? You should not rub your eyes, Fanny. The sleep will scratch them.

Sarah *puts one hand on a hip, and* **Fanny** *drifts out, still thinking of the Orinoco.*

Well, oh, well. That sunlight is a prayer in itself.

She busies herself with her bonnet.

John *in his workshop. He is humming a tune, very content. He likes the mornings. He puts on his ladling gloves, takes the wax-ladle off its peg. Approaches the wax-fire, holding the ladle out in front of him like a weapon.*

John (*amusing himself*) Nor shall my sword sleep in my hand.
(*Goes off. A little clatter of tin. Reappears with a smoking ladle.*) To
every saint his wickedness. (*Positions himself for ladling the candles,
lets the wax flow down the first wick.*) This coat for Sarah. (*The next.*)
This for Hannah. (*The next.*) This for Fanny. (*The next.*) This for
Jess. (*The next, hesitates.*) Well, this for Charity. (*Looking at
remaining candles.*) Who these others are I do not know. (*Addressing
them.*) I do not suppose you do know yourselves? I will give you
coats anyhow. For it is such weather.

Bright early morning, the pier. A long white-wooden rowing-boat, **Mr
Moore***'s.* **Fanny** *and* **Jesse** *in the bow seat,* **Mr Moore** *centre with
oars. Their good town coats,* **Mr Moore** *more anciently dressed.*
Hannah *and* **Sarah** *on the pier.* **Hannah** *holds a big armful of her
honeysuckle.*

Sarah Mr Moore, you are sure there will be no sudden
gustiness?

Mr Moore Very likely.

Sarah Very likely yea, or very likely nay?

Fanny Mr Moore is an expert at this crossing, Aunty, do enter
the boat. Me and Jesse are like two shifting horses here. There is
a whole morning in the town if you will just please get in, Aunty.

Hannah Mr Moore, where shall I put my flowers, of your
kindness?

Mr Moore (*rising*) Well (*Holding out his arms.*), I will give them to
Mr Jesse Hawke.

Hannah *steps forward with the flowers.*

Sarah If you please, Hannah, do not go trusting there. The pier
has a little coat of greenness. It is only waiting for you to
surrender your balance.

Hannah Well, hold my coat at the rear. (**Sarah** *does, unnecessarily.*) It is all right, Mr Moore (*He has shown no worry.*), I do not intend to bury you in flowers. I have a string about them.

Mr Moore Ah, good for you, Miss Hawke.

He takes them, sets them in front of **Jesse** *and* **Fanny**. *He assists* **Hannah** *into the stern seat.*

Sarah (*hopelessly, to* **Fanny** *and* **Jesse**) She is very efficient. Since I have no butter this time, I will be better staying.

Hannah Sarah. Do not let me wander about Baltimore alone. I do not want to be taken by pirates, do I, Jesse? The sea is perfectly courteous and flat today, is it not, Mr Moore?

Mr Moore Very likely.

Hannah Sarah, dear, behold. See for thyself. Between here and the town is a gentleman's dinnerplate.

Sarah Naturally I will come. (*Stamps her foot.*) I will come, (*Stamps.*) I will come.

Fanny Think of Pearse's, Aunty.

Sarah *launches herself.* **Mr Moore** *and* **Hannah** *help her to her place beside* **Hannah.**

Sarah Oh, my world.

She adjusts her bonnet, looks very pleased now.

A silly old woman.

Matt Purdy *appears above, shaking a light sunlight across them.*

Matt Purdy It was best to bring them away out of Manchester, in that white ship, upon the hilly sea. Our friend was the full of time, our foe the slight nature of our numbers. What was to be if ever there were none to marry? That was the dark figure in my dream. Oh lend us endurance, thou, Mount Gabriel. Lend us long strength, thou, Bay of Roaringwater. And, ye, little gathered islands, lend us the future of children.

He mingles back into the general light. Creak of boat. **Mr Moore** *is slowly rowing them, across the channel. The mingle and plates of water.* **Sarah** *jubilant.*

Hannah Is it not lovely now, Sarah, love?

Sarah Oh, a very special treat for an old dame.

Hannah Mr Moore is a famous rower, are you not?

Mr Moore (*smiling*) Very likely.

Fanny Mr Moore was given the prize of a ticking-clock at the Cape Clear rowing races.

Mr Moore Oh.

Hannah And did you have to accept it in Erse, Mr Moore?

Mr Moore I had to row in Erse, let me tell you.

Streaming light and water. **Jesse** *trails his hand.*

Hannah (*to* **Sarah**) I do not like to leave the people long without flowers.

Sarah Oh, I agree. Um, hum, hum.

Hannah I do hope you will bring such flowers to my resting-spot, Fanny?

Fanny I would not leave a gardener without her flowers. (*To* **Jesse**.) Do you see the curtain of light hanging there? It seems to travel along.

Jesse There is a phenomenon similar to this, under the North Pole. It is called the Aurora Borealis.

Mr Moore The Northern Lights. And I saw them.

Jesse Ah, to measure such a thing.

Mr Moore You don't care to measure them, Mr Hawke. You are leaning on the ship's rail. Your coat sticks to it with a glue of pure ice. It is the dark of the night, when the world is a whale and you are Jonah. Overhead, clear through the black spars, that wonderful sheeting of strange light. You think of your God.

Hannah And quite correctly. (*Nods at* **Sarah**.)

Sarah Oh, yes.

Hannah There are many points of similarity between us, Mr Moore, as between this, this light that Fanny saw, and that, that Aura you mention. I have always said it.

Sarah You are an excellent rower, Michael Moore.

Mr Moore I thank you. In Mayo they call that (*Indicating light.*) veins. (**Hannah** *showing polite interest.*) Yes, veins.

The curtain of light falls around **Mr Moore**.

(*As if alone.*) In particular if I could have the crow at my command I would be most thankful. In particular if I could have the robin. In particular if I could have the whistler at my command, and the warbler and the croaker, and the cryer and the caller, and the weak-throated, I would show my gratitude. Oh, yes. In particular, the shallow-rooted bush, the wind-haggard, the frost-nipped, the fluent sea-grass, the ruckled dunes, the stranded fish, in particular the long-beaked sandbird, in particular these at my command would cause in me gratitude. Oh who is the farmer of these acres, who is the farmer of these acres?

Everything as before, the light moving on.

I thank you, I thank you.

Baltimore. The town goes up above the wharf. Long blocks of shadows from the half-risen sun. **Mr Moore** *helps out* **Sarah** *and* **Hannah**, *who wait on the wharf with a certain public air. He hands up honeysuckle,* **Fanny** *and* **Jesse** *climb out. There is a quietness about them all, below* *the town. They would prefer to whisper.* **Mr Moore** *ties his rope to a ring on the wharf.*

Hannah We will go up soon to the upper street. We will make the briefest of pilgrimages now.

Mr Moore *returns to his boat, tends a clay pipe.* **Sarah** *catches* **Hannah**'s *eye.*

We will have our good time in Pearse's, never you fear. (*Leading* **Sarah** *away a little.*) Let us examine a few examples at the greatest leisure possible.

Sarah (*hushed*) If we saw a linen that we liked. Sober-dyed, mind you.

Hannah It will be our adventure.

Mr Moore (*to himself*) A pipe is as tender as a bird's leg. Tap not thy pipe.

Hannah The old must have adventures. Old maids in particular.

Sarah Oh!

Hannah (*coming back a little*) Michael, if you wished to wait for us in the hotel? You might find that cold waiting.

Mr Moore Ah, I'm much the happiest here by myself. I'll puzzle out my own concerns. Partly by philosophy, partly by daydream.

A yew-coloured light. The graveyard. **Fanny** *and* **Jesse** *wait for them.*

Hannah The holy couples.

Sarah They are always here.

Hannah They have found some peace for themselves by this sea.

Sarah (*attentive*) They have.

Hannah (*quietly, to* **Sarah**) Charity. (*Laying some of the honeysuckle.*) Sherkin has not its Charity now. She is with her wains there. That is what she wanted. My, do you recall the commotion when Fanny was born living, after these two damp boys?

Sarah *takes some honeysuckle and kneels at another spot.*

Sarah I must give old Matt Purdy a good dose of these. (*Finding something.*) Why, Hannah, a feather. I should think a starling's feather. Or a corncrake. But that needs corn. It hides itself away, in the harvest, and crakes before night.

Hannah Indeed.

Sarah (*risen*) I have greened my knees.

Hannah Look at this long root here, growing in my mother's grave. (*It is* **Mr Moore**'s *rope.*) What tree is it from?

Sarah One of the yews. A yew will walk yards from its place.

Hannah I must pull it out.

Sarah You will not pull that root out.

Hannah (*hauling*) How hard they hold.

Sarah Have a care for your back.

She puts a hand on **Hannah**'s *back.*

Around them gathers Pearse's general shop. Materials, rolls and lengths, Hawke's candles, tins, boxes, cliffs of buckets, axes, coats, boots, marked wooden drawers, bottles. The two women rise up in wonder, taking it all in. **Fanny** *and* **Jesse** *smile at them.* **Hannah** *goes forward to the counter. There is a round box there, ribbons of all sorts spill from it.*

Hannah Even this old bell I like. Will we bang a bell?

Sarah Wonders. It is all girlhood here.

Sarah *creeps to the middle of the floor vigorously.* **Meg** *comes out to them, putting up her gold hair in a loose tie.*

Meg A best of days to you all. Isn't that sunlight now, for September?

Hannah Why, it is, Meg. It is.

Meg You would make a mighty bellringer, Hannah. If there's ever a vacancy in the tower.

Hannah (*laughing*) I know! (*Turning.*) Approach, Sarah, approach. Never be timid near linens. (**Sarah** *comes up beside her, by the ribbons.*) What would you like Meg Pearse to show you?

Sarah Dark cotton! That good stuff with a hint of oats in it, of the Carolinas.

She lays a hand on the counter, not looking at it, her fingers mingle with the ribbons. **Fanny** *and* **Jesse** *find a dark corner of the shop where they poke about.* **Fanny** *draws* **Jesse**'s *notice to* **Sarah**'s *hand.* **Meg** *lands a roll of cloth on the counter.*

Meg Do you think a fisherman would give me a job? Landing fish like that?

Hannah I cannot see why he would not.

Sarah *inches in, feels the cloth.*

Meg That's what my mother used to call an easy cloth. I made a funeral dress out of that myself.

Hannah (*making a doubtful face*) Oh.

Sarah English.

Meg (*impressed*) How did you tell?

Sarah It is lighter and yet stronger than an American.

Meg Towh, Sarah, you are an expert.

Hannah She is a wonder at cloths, yes.

Sarah London-milled.

Meg *turns again.*

Meg (*pulling down roll*) Here is my dark blue. (*Landing the cloth.*) I have rarely had a cloth so rich, and it isn't pricy. I sell this to the nuns also. They make the laundry dresses from it, for the poor girls. But it's a superlative cloth just the same. American as you can wish. Those Americans know how to pack their goods. The cloths don't seem to know they've passed the wild Azores. The cloths think this is New York here.

Sarah (*feeling it*) It has a slight lustre that is agreeable.

Hannah Very fine. Of course, I am no expert like Sarah. It is extravagant for laundry girls, no? Will you show us something of that dark red?

Fanny *has found a roll of tin. She shows it to* **Jesse** *and they pretend it is a spyglass, looking through it magnificently.* **Meg** *lands the last cloth.*

Meg You don't have John with you? Or I'd call Stephen in. He's away up the top of the scallion yard.

Hannah Not this time.

Sarah *is again half at the ribbons.* **Meg** *and* **Hannah** *wait for her to say something. A bit of a gap.*

Meg And will you select a ribbon?

Sarah (*taking her hand away, laughing*) No, no! Oh, Hannah, save a friend.

Hannah You could take a black one.

Meg Look at this quality. This is a pinnacle of fashion. A stranger would speak French to you, if you wore this on your head.

Sarah Oh, no, no!

Hannah (*laughing*) Oh, Sarah, take one short ribbon in your pocket.

Sarah (*looks to* **Fanny**, *a hand one side of her mouth*) Oh, they are tormenting me, Fanny.

Meg Fanny, come over here into the light of the door and let me see you.

Fanny *hurries over.* **Meg** *grips her shoulders and looks her up and down.*

What a perfect person you are. (**Fanny** *laughing with* **Hannah**.) I am all the better for seeing you. Now give me a hug. Well, Jesse,

I won't embrace you, because you are a gentleman these last years.

Stephen Pearse *puts his head in.*

Stephen Where's that bear?

Jesse *looks about for a bear.* **Hannah** *and* **Sarah** *look at* **Stephen**, *arrested.*

Ah. Is there no John with you? (**Hannah** *shakes head.*) Ah. There's Jesse Hawke. I had something for you, Jess, I have it deep in my pockets here. (*Takes out newspaper item.*) Have yourself a cool look at that, sir. (**Jesse** *reads.*) Isn't that the most unlikely thing, Mr Jesse? I should think so.

Meg (*very kindly*) We've a little bit to do here, Stephen, you don't mind?

Stephen I'm out away again. I'm out away. I'm hoeing like the devil's own maid. But I'm halving worms mostly and I suppose this will bring us more worms. Let us hope they're decent earthworms and not chaps to eat my scallions. (**Jesse** *hands back the item.*) What do you make of that?

Jesse A deep curiosity. How do you say that, Armagh?

Stephen You have it, Armagh, Armagh.

Fanny What was in that little paper, Jesse?

Jesse They have telescopes in Armagh, Armagh, at the house of a gentleman called Johnson, and they've been digging for to make a new tower there, for a fine new Holland instrument.

Stephen That's the cold fact of it. The magic they've found there, under the old foundations, is the bones of an old animal, maybe there your million years, and they are the poor withershins and arms of an old bear.

Jesse There were bears that walked in Ireland once, Fanny. One time you might have met a bear, in Ireland.

Stephen There you have it. Well, let me extract myself. It was a joy to see you all so shipshape in my shop. God keep you.

Sarah Is that John you call a bear?

Stephen Yes, indeed, Sarah Purdy, in compliment only.

Sarah Oh, of course. Yes, yes, a bear is apt.

Stephen Be sending him now Stephen Pearse's wishes.

Sarah *smiles.*

Scallions!

He's gone.

Fanny Meg, we are looking for some sheets of paper, for Jesse, for his drawing.

Meg Paper. Paper. Why, two doors down, Fanny, my dove. Why, we have a new printer now in Baltimore. That's style for you. He'll have paper, dotey.

Jesse Who is the new man, Meg?

Meg Excuse me, Jesse?

Jesse The new man. He is not too fierce?

Meg Ah, no.

Hannah Bring Jesse down, Fanny. Here is a few coppers.

They go to door.

Meg He's a big gentle fellow. Tell him I sent you. Ah, fierce, no, no. It's Patrick Kirwin his name is.

They are gone.

(*To* **Hannah** *instead.*) From Cork City.

Hannah *responds vaguely. She looks to make sure* **Fanny** *and* **Jesse** *are gone. She beckons* **Sarah** *closer. The three heads.* **Meg** *expectant.*

Hannah Buttons!

Outside the lithographer's shop. A young woman singing. **Fanny** *and* **Jesse** *listening simply.*

Singer (*with a poor voice, but strongly*)

Are you Aurora, or the beauteous Flora, Euterpasia, or Venus
bright?
Or Helen fair, beyond compare, that Paris stole from her
Grecian's sight?

Fanny *gives her one of the coins.*

Singer (*proudly*) May God bless you.

Fanny Yes.

The lithographer's shop. A table with a lithographic stone. A high window. Dusty, familiar. **Patrick** *is busy smoothing the stone. His hand is white with dust.* **Fanny** *and* **Jesse** *peacefully watch him. He nods at them. He smiles.*

Patrick First stone in the new place!

Jesse (*after a moment*) That is wonderful.

Patrick Aye, aye. It is. See the holes in my hands? (*Shows them.*) What do you think did that?

Jesse I do not know, sir.

Patrick (*indicating walls*) Whitewash!

Noise of bee coming in through the high window. **Patrick** *fixes on it.*

Tell me, friends, what is it about Baltimore that has it plagued with bees? That's the ninth bee this good morning.

Fanny Oh, it is the nuns at the back of the town. They keep bees for wax and honey.

Patrick Ah. Good Catholic bees.

Fanny (*awkward*) Yes.

Jesse (*pointing at stone*) What is your work there?

Patrick Lithography. I suppose, rural lithography now. In Cork City I was lithographer to a newspaper. The Examiner. You read that, I'm sure.

Jesse We never see newspapers.

Fanny We never have news.

Patrick Ah, you're right. There's no good use to them. This is for a land notice. Rural, you see.

Jesse Are there no land notices in a city?

Patrick Oh, maybe, maybe. But I was at other things, from city gatherings to murders.

Jesse *intrigued.*

Well, when a man is murdered, an artist is sent out to draw the corpse. The corpse, in an attitude of terror. You see? The artist brings back the document, I smooth my stone, a stone like this one here, and I do it out for him. I do it out. (*Marking the imaginary picture.*) A hundred, a thousand impressions of the murder can be made in this way. The world sees it, the world understands the look of murder. By means of such a stone. It isn't a gentle craft, that newspaper craft. (*Brightening.*) A stone like this comes from but the one quarry in the whole world. It's in Germany, the quarry. Think of that. Well, I was mightily tired of murders. Here, around Baltimore, land notices, nice black letters, and a rare ship's notice. Much better, much. (*Lays his hand almost on the stone.*) It would be soft like a dream stone if I touched it. But I mustn't grease it. It is devious, devious. There can be a score of drawings made from this stone, if I will only smooth it, smooth it. Ah, it is a pleasure. Let me tell you (**Fanny** and **Jesse** *drawing close.*), there are little creatures held forever in this stone. Sea creatures the size of your nails, little fishes. In the quarry, on big stones, they sometimes find an old dogfish!

Fossils, fossils. When I come to a fossil, I tell it the world misses it greatly. You see, I have fled the murders!

The **Singer** *begins again.*

Do you hear that? She has been at it all morning.

Fanny That is a dance, I think. I know the steps to it.

Patrick Oh, dance it. I will be up on these local dances then. I'll be a terror at a dance by surprising everyone.

Fanny It is not a dance like that. It is only a religious dance.

Patrick I'd be honoured to see a religious dance. It'll be a blessing for my new life here in this shop.

Jesse *encourages her.* **Fanny** *dances, a stiff circular walking dance. The* **Singer** *stops.* **Fanny** *holds motionless.*

Singer (*outside*) Sir, thanking you. Sir, thanking you.

Singer *takes up song,* **Fanny** *goes into dance again.* **Patrick** *and* **Jesse** *encouraging. The song finishes.*

Fanny Now I am damp as a pony.

Jesse *puts a hand on her back.*

Patrick (*fanning the bee away from himself*) We've stirred up that wild lad of the nuns.

The bee goes to **Jesse**.

Jesse If you stand perfectly still you are safe.

Bee goes to **Fanny**. *She cannot help shooing it away. It stings her hand.*

Fanny Now, look at that. What a biter he is, that little bee.

Patrick (*coming around to her*) The savage.

Fanny But it will die now. It was my doing.

Patrick *peers at her hand.*

I am sorry for the Catholic bee.

Patrick (*to* **Jesse**) My room in the back there, my kitchen. Will you fetch me the bottle of vinegar there?

Jesse *hurries away.*

I'm sorry to touch your hand.

Fanny *smiles.*

Patrick I have to draw out the sting, you see. Would you look at my own paw. (*He means the white dust on it. Some of it transfers to hers.*) Alas, I have no instrument for this.

He works to get the sting out with his nails, close to her hand. **Fanny** *watches his crown. He goes down on one knee. They are silent. He draws out the sting. He looks up at her to speak. Sees her watching. A moment together.* **Jesse** *returns.*

Jesse What is vinegar?

Fanny *laughs.*

Patrick Ho, mercy. Well, of course, vinegar is a mystery to some. My mother was a Lisbon woman, a Jewish woman, that my father brought home to marry. (*Realises his own proposing position, rises, confused.*) She spoke three tongues, the Portuguese, the Hebrew, and the Cork. She was the sort of person that likes vinegar in her supper. And so do I.

Fanny Where is your mother?

Patrick My mother? She has a stone house. You understand me? The star of David and the cross of Jesus are cut there on it. I did that, though it isn't my trade.

Fanny (*rubbing her hand*) Thank you.

Patrick Yes, yes.

Fanny Do you have some nice paper, it would be for Jesse, he charts out the travels of the stars there in the sky above our Sherkin, and he needs a good plain paper without wax.

Patrick I can manage that. (*To* **Jesse**.) I suppose you have a good spyglass British-made for your observances?

Jesse (*regretful*) No.

Patrick No matter. I have paper with a little English watermark. It is the best paper in this world. I hope that will suit you!

Fanny and **Jesse** *laughing*. **Patrick** *winks*.

Aye.

Mr Moore, *alone with his boat. He sings a few lines of a marriage song in Irish.*

Mr Moore (*musing*) Valparaiso. To think of all the sailors that have whispered a prayer passing Cape Clear, the last of Europe's land. And they were never on it once. And yet I've seen its fine lighthouse, talked to that keeper, a man who knows how dark and gold his sea may be. There is a barracks there full of Lancashire boys. And some weighty houses, and a school by a stony beach where the children murmur their new words. And a fine harbour, and green roads and brave sorts of figures in those houses, men that fear fathoms too. It's odd to think of all those heartfelt prayers directed there, by sailors growing lonely. And all unknowing the people in the houses. Such tenderness. Valparaiso. (*After a moment.*) Ah, dear sailors. How simple the heart becomes at the head of a long voyage, a cargo of coals out of Cardiff maybe, to go round Cape Horn to San Francisco. Through lightning that melts the little weather-cock on the high mast. Molten stars strike the deck! The men in the yards find the ends of their fingers charred. Dear sailors, simple, leaving aft the prayers of Cape Clear. Ah, human men. I know the words myself. (*Mouths a half-silent prayer, with a gesture of goodbye.*) Go dtugadh Dia slán abhaile sinn.[1] I suppose in their time a few prayers have missed Cape Clear and washed against Sherkin.

[1] May God bring us safely home.

The prayers of Sherkin would be firewood of that sort.
Valparaiso. Tháinig long ó Bhalparésó.[2] And so on. Valparaiso.

Hannah, **Sarah** *with a little parcel*, **Fanny** *and* **Jesse** *with his roll of paper, descend towards him.* **Sarah** *and* **Jesse** *tip their purchases against each other.* **Mr Moore** *bestirs himself.*

Ah, here they come, my stormy petrels.

A simple music. A scattering.

Evening, the same day. **John** *is struggling in his workshop to set up a separate candle-making frame. He attaches to it one long wick. He is ready. He takes the ladle.* **Fanny** *comes in. He brightens.*

Fanny Father, we are home again.

He gets the glove on his free hand by sticking it under his oxter. He touches her face.

John Were you away someplace, child?

Fanny We were in the shining capital of Baltimore.

John (*going off, clatter of stove and ladle*) Is it an object of envy, this head?

Fanny Sarah has her three-day soup.

John (*returning with filled ladle*) Ho, that three-day soup.

Fanny It is your time to come home, if you wished. (*Touches his arm.*)

John *winks and nods. He stands on his stool, lets the first wax flow down the wick.*

John This is the blessed candle for the nuns. It is the Easter candle. There will be true gold bound to it, and they will set in

[2] A ship came from Valparaiso.

blue lines made from a store of lapis lazuli. And they will hoard it nicely till April and even then it will only burn in the bowel of their mansion. They will watch over it zealously. It will be their candle.

Fanny They are always happy with their candle.

John And it is a tricky thing to make a nun happy, I think.

Fanny They are reasonable little women.

John Oh, they are wonders. There is an ancientness about them that in a light way appeals. That dress of theirs with the blackened cloth and the hoops of cowls like big lilies, you know what that is, Fanny?

Fanny I think I might, Father.

John It is something from a medieval world. Among nuns you may be in the twelfth century still. They are the opposite of women of fashion. And yet they are highly fashionable among the scattered people.

Fanny They have a stronger world.

John I do not mind nuns. No. I think they are waiting also over there, the back of the lighted town. It might be that we would meet them in any New Jerusalem, since they are happy nuns.

Fanny They will look strange in the bright new streets.

John Strange women enough, but an adornment.

Fanny It is not just we three families then always? And extra brothers, if whatever, from Manchester?

John Who will say that? Not I.

Considers his work.

Fanny It is a famished-looking candle at this moment.

John Oh, I have yards and months of ladling to do. I will do it piecemeal when the spirit takes me. It is a special task for me, because of course we depend on them for wax, year by year. I

could not quarrel with a nun here. The next site of wax is by
Cork City I believe, and that is a lengthy way. You would be
heaped up in a cart five days to Cork City, and be thoroughly
rained on. And it is a decent sort of wax, the nuns' wax. If we
did not live on an island of winds, we might manage our own.

Fanny Father, in your prayer, when you prayed for a husband –

John Yes, Fanny? (*Stepping down, setting aside ladle. Off with his
gloves.*) Did I not pray correctly?

Fanny You did, Father. I understand you. Oh, Father, I am lost
in my feeling for Matt Purdy. I wish that I had met him.

John (*putting his hands each side of her face. His hands are a little gritty
from the gloves*) Charity and I were late with our work, my heart's
child. Old Purdy was terribly elderly, even when I was young.
He stepped in his own time, and was not for you, it seems. But
he was a man of splendid eyes. His face was as soft as yours all
his life, his hair rose up in a pleasant mass of flames. He was a
curious seer. Our perfect father.

Fanny He led the families here, Father.

John He did, Fanny.

Fanny Father, let me tell you. In the town today there was a
man, he was a pleasant, a pleasant-tongued man, from Cork
City. He is the lithographer, the new figure in the town. (**John**
shows he may have heard of him.) Father, as I watched him, my cold
body stirred, I was moved towards him.

John Easy, easy, child. You may be easy. You are a clear
person. It is wished by God that a person makes her children.
You are a savage little mother, you, Fanny. Yes. It is far older
than nuns. But all present cities and towns are dark things,
which light cannot alter. It is often with an uneasy hand
(*Showing right hand.*) that I mete out my candles to Baltimore.
Am I not bringing little bundles of light to a place that light
cannot feed? But contrariwise, the town needs light, and my poor
trickle of it, maybe, can help the widow in her long night, the
child in his beforesleep. And, Fanny, a child is light.

Fanny The lithographer touched my heart, Father.

John Yes, yes, child. And he is from Cork City? Does he have his manners? Did you see what he was?

Fanny He spoke of his old life there. Some of it went hard by me. He had I think a pride for his trade, as you have, and as I have for Sherkin. He seemed to put his stony work against the difficulties of a life. He was buoyant. He had no malice, but he liked to play, with Jesse and me, in words. He thought we were donkeys, I am sure, and so we were. He rescued me, look, from a bee-sting. Oh, he was dressed in the world. He was not like us. But I knew him.

John A good man, a good man. He is a rare man. But there will come certainly a brother from England if Matt Purdy wishes it, or his abiding spirit. In good polished boots, will come that man, for you.

Fanny (*simply*) I do know, Father.

John It is an article, Fanny, that we must abide. There will be no city for us without it. Were you to go from the families, how could you return? There would be a tearing in you. To marry such a foreign sort, you would need to embrace more than him, you would need to loosen us from your arms, and embrace his beliefs.

Fanny It was a moment, Father. It is certain that he had no notion of me as a person there.

John I will tell you this, Fanny, because you are my own. I have no true hope for Jesse, no true hope. He is a kind of wonderful boy, I imagine in my soul that he is a kind of visionary, but clipped down to the earth. There is a great deal of Matt Purdy in us all, but in him greatly again. Ah, in my dreams I see no wife for Jesse. My little child, there is not anything fearful in what I say. But my prayers are that, in spite of all, a brother will come from Manchester, though we have heard nothing from there for so many years. I see him arriving, like a veritable planet, when I am asleep in the goose-bed. He is just an ordinary man, and tired from his voyage. But he comes to us plainly. And if it is unto the fourth generation that we are to abide here for the city of light, then he will come surely. I can say nothing else to you. But I know what has leaped in you. It is the gazelles of life. It is the spirit of your children, and they are as eager as you for the earth of Sherkin.

Fanny Father, I will abide.

John Dear, dear Fanny. Here in my workroom, here together in secret, in this moment of our hours, I bless you with a father's word. There is nothing to keep you with us, Fanny Hawke. The four doors of the island are open. Walk away out if you wish or must. Ah, you could not return from such a voyage, but it would be a true voyage and your own. Whatever your star is, morning or evening, you will know best. There would be a long and tedious mourning in my heart if you were to go. But I would have my own light daughter stay only in her freedom. Fanny, you are the heart's tincture and the candle of this Sherkin. When your father sees you he is proud and easy. When Hannah and Sarah and Jesse see you, they are proud and easy. Fanny Hawke is our familiar light. Every creature knows the lighthouse of Sherkin.

Fanny Father, I will abide.

Act Two

A simple music. Late evening in the town. **Meg** *in her shop, with all the quietness of the end of the day.* **Patrick** *has come in to her. He is awkward, trying to be casual. She sweeps the shop floor methodically.*

Patrick Mrs Pearse, you know me now a handful of months, less maybe, while I've been (*Smiles.*) setting up here, and to-ing and fro-ing between this paradise and the city. I have never talked to you.

Meg But you have, Mr Kirwin, in a fashion. If you think you haven't, that's since you're a very awkward man, Mr Kirwin. And I mean that in kindness, I do.

Patrick Aye. Kindness. My very theme. I could write out a school attempt at that. Kindness. I don't want to shock you with vocabulary, but kindness means in the original use, matters of family. Did you know that?

Meg I'm not a scholar, dear Mr Kirwin. I went to the Presbyterian Institute till I was ten. And then no more. Let me tell you, Mr Kirwin, it was a release. I can count and read, I cannot spell, but I'm happier now so. There was a very dreary master with a lively stick. He never beat me, but, oh, the very waving of it over your head. I never did see the point of all that conning and scholarship.

Patrick Aye. Well, look. I am a plain man. Truly, from a place like this, set within the supposed glories of Cork City. I was reared there poorly. There is nothing to recommend me to anyone. Yet I worked hard and long at my trade, and I'm fit for it. I must be the most passionate tradesman ever put his name above a lithographer's shop. That recommends me, if little else.

Meg Now, Mr Kirwin.

Patrick You are a very, a very complete person, Mrs Pearse. You are my own age and I can speak to you, at least.

Meg My God, Mr Kirwin, you must be forty, by the most diminished account. What kind of compliments are you offering me?

Patrick Ah.

Meg Never mind, I'm not so empty. What are you wanting to tell me?

Patrick Ah, you're kind, Mrs Pearse. And merciful. It is this. Here is my speech in a nutshell. I am poorly born, I am – I am awkward, as you say. To tell you all the truth, I didn't have the stomach for my work in Cork City. Too many murders, a surfeit. I was happy to lithograph the horse races, the buntings for the royal visit, the fine bits of carpentry done in the streets for it, the men elected to councils, the women that astonished the city with their feathers and their gowns. But murders, young women killed, great rows of young men and bodies after, knifings, and then, Mrs Pearse, the poor creatures down in the prisons, the women that robbed and the rope around them, the men that lost their eyes in debt and the rope around them, such things are gristly and discommoding, believe you me. A famine of charity.

Meg Credo, credo.

Patrick Look at me, Mrs Pearse. Am I company for anyone? I have got wild there in my shop. I should have linked myself to friends here. Well, I intend staying here not so long more. Certainly murders withered me, but Baltimore is driving me from what wits I had.

Meg Another astute compliment. And this is no nutshell, Mr Kirwin.

Patrick (*a touch fiercely*) There were two in my shop these few mornings past. A strange boy with a crooked throat and a resplendent girl. Well, she was more woman than girl. They are from that close island.

Meg Fanny Hawke and her brother Jesse? She is my own age,
Mr Kirwin, though she didn't school with me, being what she is.

Patrick But what is she? That is the point. What is she? She was
very, well, skimming, on the matter of Catholic bees, and I was
frightened to ask her. They are not your own allegiance?

Meg No, not hardly. They are some of those people that in
English cities concocted new religions. I suppose they were types
of the times. Previous times, since the heart is gone out of their
movement. I have heard them described variously.
Prelapsarians, Millenarians. All such names.

Patrick Millenarians? Hat-makers?

Meg No, no, that's milliners, Mr Kirwin.

Patrick Long names for such a girl. Quakers?

Meg Something in that yard of things. Visionaries. (*Taking down
a packet.*) That's them there too. Hawke's Ideal Candles.
Sixpence.

Patrick Here, give me them. (*Fetches out sixpence.*) It is beyond
me. Beyond me. You are no bigot, Mrs Pearse, or I've got
madder than I think. The truth is, she came in on me, she
washed in on me. Of course, of course, she didn't notice her
effect. She is an angel maybe, and sees no desire.

Meg Oh, I doubt that. I do. Mr Kirwin, you are telling me in
your own way that you're smitten by her?

Patrick Well, that's it.

Meg They don't marry the likes of you, or of me either. They are
tribalists – that is to say, they keep all as it was before cities and
such. I must say, they would make an outcast of Fanny Hawke if
she turned herself to you. Now, that's all I know. Believe you
me, it's a dark and difficult faith they have, and there's no real
amplitude in it. The tribes of Israel were never so odd.

Patrick Israel, Israel, yes. (*About to say something, changes his* *mind*.) You make me sweat. This isn't good. Let me introduce you to my wife, the visionary.

Meg Aren't you a sort of tribalist yourself, Mr Kirwin?

Patrick Aye, aye, so I suppose. If I let myself.

Meg Mr Kirwin, you're trembling. We like you, Mr Kirwin, because you are clear. You make a good field notice. You are pleasant and an addition to the town. But you are a little dishonest here. For wouldn't Fanny Hawke have to make another thing of herself for you, and how would that please anyone? You have wild bishops now, that wouldn't let you touch her till you'd made a pleasant little changeling of her. And what is this, but a girl you saw in the morning?

Patrick Aye. But I don't care for bishops. Bishops are just government. And I don't care for that either.

Meg Well, a very great rebel. Still, you might just let her go past you. (*Rubbing an arm, as if cold*.) Her father is very mad, I think. They seem to me all mad, in their way. Though I admit that Fanny is a good likeable person. Extremely. In fact, such an extreme is likely a poor tying for you. To balance it she is bright and funny. I'm always glad to see her. I doubt if you're the first man to feel her force. Maybe. But it's only a great mire you'd be treading into – a great mire. She has two aunts like sentinel hounds. Miss Hannah Hawke is just as her name suggests. You could hunt mice and hares with her, if you could find a hood for her head and a glove for your own hand.

Patrick I don't seem to mind any of that. I think I'd risk the murder. And someone else could draw me on a stone. Mrs Pearse, I'm in a quandary now. You've talked a yard of sense. I'll try to let it go past, as you say. I will try. A wind in the bushes.

Meg You were good to come and talk to me, Mr Kirwin. You don't need to hesitate again. We like you. Mr Pearse likes you, though we hie to different churches on a Sunday.

Patrick Aye.

A brief wave with the hand holding the candles. He goes out looking at the packet. **Stephen Pearse** *comes in from the house. He carries with him a hand of scallions.*

Stephen Am I too late for him, Meg?

Meg For who is that, darling?

Stephen Wasn't that my big bear of a friend, John Hawke? He's going away there in the darkness. That's certainly himself. Let me call him back for a little parley.

Meg That's only the poor lithographer. Let him be, with his new thoughts.

Stephen Haven't they the same back, the very selfsame cut to them, those two?

Meg Oh, a miracle. But Patrick Kirwin might steal from John Hawke, for all that their backs are the same.

Stephen How so, Meg, how so?

Meg Ah, he's in talking, talking. One of those Hawke women has him spinning. Men in love are mules.

Stephen Not Hannah. Not Sarah!

Meg Fanny, dear, Fanny.

Stephen Fanny Hawke is a child.

Meg She isn't, dear. (*Smiling.*) She is my own age.

Stephen By God. (*After a bit.*) There's no marrying outside for them, is there, Meg?

Meg No more than ourselves.

Stephen That's true, that's true. (*Knocking the scallions on the counter vaguely.*) He's a nice old person, John, I wouldn't care to see him troubled. By such a mere city man too. But no danger of that, no danger of that, not in our close world.

Meg *makes her face show otherwise.*

Perhaps I will hint to him when I go out ordering candles. Perhaps I will do that, now. A few choice words, to John.

Meg Perhaps you'll leave it alone. I told seven white lies and put Patrick Kirwin out of his frenzies. He isn't such a terrible city man. He's a bit of a honey, now, like your own honeyed self. Look at you, with those poor scallions.

Stephen I think our friends the worms have got the best half of these jobs. Those worms are just wild characters, aren't they, and eager for their unjust share. Every poor hanged villain comes back into the world as a worm, and they're all up there in that yard, yarning away about the old killing days, and taking bites out of these between speeches. By God. Are they no good to you, sweety?

Meg Well, I'll give them a good chop with a knife, and kill off any wormy remains in a fierce stew.

Stephen Ah, you will, you will, and why wouldn't you? They showed no mercy themselves when they were murdering men. I was three months of a summer growing those.

Meg My dear old gardener, sure.

Stephen I am, come here to me.

Meg (*going to him*) Is that my name now, come-here-to-me?

Stephen Isn't it a lovely perfect name? Lean there on my breast, Meg.

Meg Ah, I will for a minute. I'm fond of this breast.

Stephen It's an old breast.

Meg It would look fine enough in a goose-bed. I have just such a bed upstairs, here, in my husband's shop.

Stephen Is it just up there? I seem to know the way.

Patrick *juts in.* **Stephen** *would pull away but* **Meg** *holds him.*

Patrick Mercy me, friends. But the sixpence.

He spins it, bright and new, across the shadows of the shop. **Meg** *catches it.* **Patrick** *is gone again.*

A simple music. The moon over Sherkin, a sickle. It grows to fullness. It's three weeks later. Dawn, a clear spread light. The whitethorn a little barer. **Mr Moore** *leaning, smoking, enjoying the morning, a little way off the pier. The thin smoke drifts upward. (In the shadows of* **John***'s workshop, the Easter candle is somewhat fatter.)* **Eoghan O Drisceoil** *rises from his currach, with a thick net over his shoulder.*

Eoghan A land with a little hotel. There is no high path to the farms, no green road to the middle farms, no metalled road to the school. There is no beach of large round stones with ragged children. There is no brace of soldiers walking redly. There is no kirk, (*Playing with the word.*) kirk. But it's a simple yellow land with some peace attached to it. I can love my Clear Island. Sherkin I can love too.

Takes out his bone-needle and squats on pier to work. **Mr Moore** *taking cognisance of him.*

(*To* **Mr Moore**. *He speaks English with almost a Scandinavian accent.*) You're early here.

Mr Moore I brought a man over early. I didn't know him. From the city maybe. O Drisceoil is your name, is it not?

Eoghan It is. I am taking advantage of this fine flat surface on your new pier, and the lack of crowds.

Mr Moore Oh.

Silent for a bit. Peaceful.

Any sharks this year out at your island?

Eoghan Not this year.

Mr Moore I saw a shark myself in the summer sea by the Rock of Filth. Another man caught one under Fastnet. You've fewer in October. Shark meat. Did you ever eat that?

No response.

It's the same as eating courage.

Eoghan Who was it caught that shark?

Mr Moore A man out of Bantry.

Eoghan Is that it?

Mr Moore Very likely.

Eoghan (*spotting* **Fanny** *coming down the track*) Here is a little monk.

Mr Moore *looks, waits for her to reach him.*

Mr Moore Good morning, Fanny Hawke.

Fanny Good morning, Mr Moore.

Eoghan Dia is Muire dhuit.[1]

Fanny I would like to greet you in your proper language, sir, but I do not have it. My brother has it, a little.

Eoghan Ah, there isn't anything in it. It is just an old tongue. It isn't so great in the world as your own babble. It's a creaking tongue, spoken by a rusty people. (**Mr Moore** *laughing*.) We're much rained on, out there, on the sea. We're gatherers of rain. So you needn't mind it.

Fanny You are very generous about it. I know well from Jesse what it is. He says it is a language of voyages, and of fighting.

Eoghan Jesse, is that his handle? Lord God. And he should know about fighting, a thief of his renown.

Fanny *doesn't understand him.* **Eoghan** *shakes his head, laughs a little oddly.*

[1] God and Mary be with you. (common greeting)

Hah. I leave all fighting to the English soldiers. It is easier, and they like that better. They get the potatoes with the black eyes from us. They're blind potatoes. It isn't any good to feed such potatoes to a woman with child. She may bear a bat.

Fanny You are not a fighter but a fisherman.

Eoghan There are fish too that are fighters, and fish that are not. A mackerel is a pugilist, whereas a pollack makes a weight of himself but never stirs a muscle in his own defence.

Mr Moore I often noted that.

Eoghan That's it. What protects him best is that he's not the best eating. The mackerel is an oily fellow but he puts flesh on the devourer. But pollack in a pie is my dish, and my mother's dish.

Fanny Is that how you have it over there? You are as wise as Jesse on the fishes.

Eoghan Your Jesse has a deal to say and it's all sense. And we thought he was in Mexico! But I like a man that can talk to a foreigner with his own few words.

Fanny You are not a foreigner.

Eoghan I am a foreigner on Sherkin. That's why I like it.

Fanny And myself?

Eoghan You are a foreign woman at home here.

Fanny *laughs*.

Fanny I am informed.

Eoghan Aye. Don't mind me.

Fanny *moves away again*.

Tell your outlaw his secret is safe with me.

Fanny *looks to* **Mr Moore** *for clarity*. **Mr Moore** *shrugs*.

There's something Sherkin has that we don't. (*Working his net.*) An outlaw.

Mr Moore How do you mean that, an outlaw?

Eoghan Ah, I got a little book off a soldier. The Only True History of Frank James, by Himself. There was good reading in it. He was robbing railroads there, with his brother, Jesse, in America.

Mr Moore (*after a moment*) And what happened to them?

Eoghan Ah, some say they're in Mexico, and some others say they're in South America. The main thing is, according to my book, they're alive. They got away.

Mr Moore Valparaiso.

Eoghan (*after a moment*) Maybe so, maybe so.

Patrick *arriving at the whitethorn. Previous scene gone. He seems to hang about, very uncertain. Looks around him, then puts himself in against the whitethorn and unbuttons his flies.*

Patrick You'd think I'd be spared the tyranny of the bladder for once.

Waits, looks down, nothing happening.

Christ, the reluctant suitor.

Jesse *passes the other side of the tree, carrying the broom to work. He spots the unexpected figure, brandishes broom,* **Patrick** *hurries to fasten his flies.*

Jesse Leave away, man in the bush!

Patrick *raises a hand to calm him, but finds he needs it more for his flies.*

Patrick Mister, mister, you know me.

Jesse What evil are you bringing to my tree?

Patrick The little crossing in the boat has put the tea through me.

Jesse Oh, step away back from that innocent whitethorn!

Patrick I'm clear, I'm clear. Do you see who it is? I am Patrick Kirwin, that sold you paper.

Jesse (*calmer*) I suppose it is. Yes, I know you.

Patrick I've hurried over between storms.

Jesse You had better hurry back. There is a long black storm preparing.

Patrick I have the last room of the year at the hotel. I tell you, it's an hotel for rats.

Jesse So we hear. (*Leaning on broom.*) I have never been.

Patrick The sheets are like the yellow leaves off the big plants in the Botanical Gardens in Glasgow. Do you think I haven't seen them? I have, like elephants' ears, sir.

Jesse (*letting the broom swing in his hand like a pendulum*) I am sorry for your comfort. This is not a holidaying island. The hotel is a night-house for whatever travelling persons come to see us, to sell us stuff, as may be, or glories that do break in a day. Gentlemen that do hail from the East and hurry back there, I tell you, when their goods are tested by this island. I suppose we put a bend in most things. The odd stray bird stays there in that hotel, and even they in a morning look dishevelled and tormented on the pier, as if they had slept with lions like Daniels. Your owner there is properly a seaweed collector. That is his yearly work.

Patrick It's no matter. I've no interest in comfort for now. We've met very awkwardly here, Jesse, but, have charity, and take a word for me to Fanny.

Jesse (*holding the broom steady*) For what use, stranger?

Patrick I want you to take a word to her, for to meet me, under that hotel when she wishes, by the blank blind wall. (*Tentatively.*)

I will wait there, Jesse, it is where my present window looks out on a waste of scrubby rock. Mr Hawke, dear, even I can see winter out there, the sea is blackening, it has an army out there in those waves. There are white waves like a stand of bitter trees, God help us, there is smoke and wild white leaves mixed wildly. Will you carry that word for me, boy?

Jesse (*brandishing the broom*) I may. I may.

Patrick To your sister, Jesse.

Jesse (*angry*) I know to who. My sister is my own. She is our own. (*Shakes his head like a sweating boxer.*)

Patrick Your father I know has a tongue of terror, (**Jesse** *puzzled by this, lets it go by.*) – I know, or I would ask him. Did Mrs Pearse tell me right?

Jesse (*threatening with the broom*) She is not your kind, man.

Patrick I haven't so much to say. I haven't a speech. Will you have her come?

Jesse (*giving up*) You do not understand me. Did you never see an ant stepped on? It is a very slight death.

Patrick I won't stay beyond a night.

Jesse I wonder what you will make of one of our island nights.

Jesse *goes on with the broom. The bare, poor hotel room gathers about* **Patrick**, *at first darkly, then a thin light of early morning. He has not slept. The bed.*

Patrick There are fish in the mortar of this wall and they are not fossils. It is that damp, they're swimming around in it. I have been in Glasgow, where they have many cheap hotels for cheap travellers. Pity, pity to the man who must spend his life in such a room as this. (*Rubbing his face, scratching his thigh.*) I thought I'd had my allotment of fleabites in this life. I was brother to many generations of fleas in my youth. Well, that's how we lived. There isn't any need for nobility. I will never keep a cat. That's the most vicious fleas. I think Fanny Hawke has a clear head. I think she is much the best, much the best. Still, I never saw one like her, so I don't know. Maybe she's a ghost. A sort of vision, in her terms. I think maybe Baltimore is a vision too. A hellish one. Of course it is myself that is the vision. Of misery. The fleas are taking great nourishment from a vision none the less. Christ, (*Trapping a flea.*) that's not a flea, that's the whole dog. Maybe it is wrong of me to take a visionary child away from her island, or seek to. But I can do no other thing. If I require to be forgiven, forgive me. I'm following only before a thing that's far wickeder and blinder than myself. Not so wicked, no, not so wicked. In this fashion I would say, I love her. Was there ever love more foolish or more forceful? I have a fire under my arse, and it isn't only made by the mouths of fleas. My head even is just a hearth. You could leave spuds in it at night and take them to school in the morning, in the frost. Christ, I am lost for this bright woman. I have to submit. (*Strikes palm on bed like a wrestler.*) I submit. Take that twist off my arm. And I will not be put away from her. I'll be greater than I am. I'll be subtle, I'll be a real dancer. No one will know me. I'll get a shock in mirrors. Ah, I'll weep wicked tears if she'll even hear me. I swear it. I'll lose my legs as well as my heart. She'll slay me. And I'll rejoice. I'll send penny cards to all my acquaintance, saying, Fanny Hawke killed me. That is the better sort of murder. And may God give me good words for her, give me words.

A few small black pebbles are thrown into the room, which at first he doesn't see. He is itchy in his legs. He leans forward and pulls up a trouserleg carefully, to see if he can spot a flea.

Oh, you have me devoured alive, you subtle devils.

Now he is a better position to see the next sequence of pebbles.

Christ, them are fleas.

He creeps over, catches a flea as it were, examines it, realises what it must be, strikes his forehead, hurries to window, looks down.

Merciful Christ.

He goes quickly from the room. Outside, **Fanny** *is throwing pebbles.*

Gulls screeching. It is a cold dank wall. She tries to see up into the
window. It's too high. She has her arm reared to throw again. **Patrick**
comes up behind her, touches her raised hand briefly. She turns, dropping
the pebbles. She is a little angry.

Fanny What is it then?

Patrick (*confused*) Aye.

Fanny Mr Kirwin.

Patrick Aye, I know. I have only half of a notion now. Well,
look at you, here. I feel myself to be a very awkward being. Well,
what is a hero? I am a lithographer, from Cork City, and a fool.
I feel like a mouse, scratching at a parlour door, and there is
only big cats inside, if he knew.

Fanny (*laughing*) A mouse?

Patrick I have been peering out my whole life for the familiar
face. (*Stops, because* **Fanny** *is puzzled.*) I have this to say to you.
Think of me now as you see me, think of me, store me in your
warm head till the spring, and I will come then and ask you to
come away with me. I know all your particular difficulties. Now,
I leave you with that. And if you are wiser, and won't come, it'll
be hard news, but I won't trouble you after.

Fanny There would not be any purpose rowing out here in the
spring, Mr Kirwin.

Patrick Yes, yes.

Fanny I am not a woman to go. We are very established
religious people here. (*Laughing.*) You cannot imagine what holds
me here. It is my life but also other lives. I am bound to this
place by family willingly.

Patrick Oh, that talk is your talk. That's what has me shivering
by this wall. There's something in you that shocks me, but only
as a piece of lightning shocks a chimney. (*A gust of wind.*) Oh, a
foolish speech. And I wonder, listening to you, if I would be
worthy of you.

A darkening over.

Fanny I like you and your mouse, Mr Kirwin. It is just that you are speaking to a woman quite given over to this other existence. It is not a life as you follow it, (*A sudden rain falling.*) I think.

Patrick And could I ever lead this life? Could I bring myself here? (*Hunching in the chill.*)

Fanny There are only three families for this place, unless you are a Manchester brother. I do not think you are.

Patrick (*mouthing*) Manchester brother. Is that something in particular? What is such a thing? (*Gives up.*) Nevertheless, you'll find me in the spring, a sort of seed-sower at the door. You will watch out for me, you think?

Rain lifts. A patch of sunlight crosses them.

Fanny Keep where you abide, Patrick Kirwin. Hold to your shop. Do not waste a sixpence for Mr Moore on me.

Patrick Aye, but he's only the thruppence.

Fanny *leaves him, heads away. She is stopped by* **Eoghan** *coming to her from the pier. He carries a frame with larger-sized shells attached to it. He holds it out to her.* **Patrick** *sunk in thought, darkening by the wall.*

Eoghan I've made for you a shell-toy. (*He hands it to her.*) If you set it right in your window, a change of wind will sound in it among the ears. (*The ground steaming after the rain, birds, scents.*) A fisherman would use it to foretell a fishing wind. But you could use it for a pleasing toy, as any Clear Island child might.

Fanny *takes it gratefully, nods her thanks, turns and carries it into the house. She places the shell-toy in a window. A simple music. By the stove are empty baskets, one full of driftwood. It is deep winter, late afternoon, the five candles are lit. The remote glow of the stove.* **John** *stands by it, with his book, intending to read to them. The whitethorn tree is bare, frosted.* **Sarah**, **Hannah**, *and* **Jesse** *ranged to hear him,* **Fanny** *sits down, just a little apart from them, thinking. A flash of lightning.*

Sarah Too bitter for me, and dark, this weather. (*Rubs her eyes.*) Dark!

The crash of the thunder overhead. **John** *stares up.*

Hannah Sarah. Nonsense.

John (*hesitant*) I have selected, I have underscored (*More confidently.*) with my black pencil, these passages following out of John of (*Flash of lightning.*) Patmos (*Fierce rain.* **John** *looks up again, silenced, waiting. Crash of thunder overhead. He goes on listening,* **Hannah** *and* **Sarah** *looking at him.*)

John *strikes away out through the storm to his workshop. His candle is further advanced.* **Stephen** *arrives in, heavily coated, shaking the rain off himself, pulling a big hat off to reveal himself.*

Stephen I've brought myself over! Good gracious, John, what a wild day. See, (*Drying his hands off, delicately taking from an inner pocket a slip of paper.*) to give you this order.

John Ah, ah.

Stephen We were going to endure a scarcity otherwise. And that wouldn't do, this closing-in weather.

Sets paper on grid. **John** *grasps his hand.*

John Stephen Pearse, too long since we met! I am full of remorse. I have made you a fresh store of candles as usual for the lighting of the town of Baltimore, and I hope that you may forgive me my not bringing them over before this late date!

Stephen *just a trifle taken aback by the force of this.*

Stephen Lay them by for us, John, and get them over when you can arrange it with Moore, and, the God of this weather.

John (*brightly*) I will do that for you, Stephen.

They shake.

Stephen I lay some store by you, John Hawke, and not just for candles.

John I know, Stephen, and it is a mutual liking. It would be hard for me in the sense of money not to bring you my candles, but even leaving that aside, and were I to find another shop, I would not be happy with it. Friendship inspires. There is a sense in which I make them for you. Hawke's candles are sold there in Pearse's, and that seems to me the fitting arrangement. It has been so for two, three generations, eh?

Stephen Yes.

They relax.

John You will abide here a little while, and dry out your nice coat?

Stephen Thank you, thank you. (*He peels off his coat, drapes it to dry.*)

John Just a second, Stephen.

He goes off to the wax-fire and comes back with two bowls of **Sarah**'s *soup.*

There is the thing now for us in this extremity.

They sit on whatever available perches. Eat.

Stephen That's a very strange affair now, in Mafeking, out beyond there, in Africa.

John *blank*.

I'll tell you something now, which I mightn't have told you, if you weren't of especial importance to me and Meg. Do you know the lithographer, Patrick Kirwin?

John No, I have never been in his shop. He is a Cork City man, I believe.

Stephen Look, John, he is a good man but he was in talking to Meg some while since, very keenly. He is taken in some manner with Fanny, and I think he would ask you for her as a wife.

John Yes, I do know. Did she tell him, Meg, what we were?

Stephen She did. He went off in the end very disappointed. She told him that Fanny was only for marrying of her kind. That you are a very strict people in your way.

John It is beginning to be a difficulty for us. It was fine just as long as we had our own husbands and wives here on the island. Poor Fanny. I cannot tell what to do for her, Stephen. But how can there be a question of permission? I have no permission to give. It was Matthew Purdy's most profound article. And he was a soft man enough. 'He that leaves the families must be outcast and outlaw, and shunned of the tribe.' It is part of his pre-Satanic vision. She must abide on the island or else she is not a daughter of our families. It perhaps sounds harsh and ill to you, Stephen?

Stephen What was done in old cases, when they went?

John Why, no one has ever left, but to the graveyard.

Stephen Things are set as they are set. I know the long vigil you've kept on Sherkin and what your business is here. So, I think Meg has thoroughly frightened off Patrick Kirwin. You might have sounded like a strange affair to him. I saw him go away very dark.

John Fanny is not fixed, nor are any of us. We are not imprisoned, why that would be the opposite of what Matt Purdy wished. But we have our own doing of things. We were only three families that fled. We are terribly reduced. It would be a terrible hurt still to lose her. She could not go in that normal fashion that people know.

Stephen He is a Catholic to boot, of course.

John Ah. It is hopeless. Why, your own son even, if he had existence, could not marry her without the same loss. Even he could not be one of us. As little, Mr Kirwin, he is not a brother. She would have to suffer a change to have him. She would cross from one condition to another. I am not the father for Patrick Kirwin. I cannot be Patrick Kirwin's father.

Stephen Well, he knows that now.

John Often I trouble myself that ours is a bitter creed. And yet it is based on kindness, on family and hope. It has been such a long waiting. I thank you for your mercy, Stephen, in seeking to discuss this with me.

Stephen Well, I revere you.

John *silenced.* **Stephen** *clothes himself. Takes* **John**'s *hand.*

Good evening to you, John.

John May Mr Moore row you carefully home.

Stephen He is a careful man.

The easy fall of waves. **Fanny** *alone, out on the edge of the strand.*

Fanny The tide of this island is a fierce tide, it could carry you. The Atlantic here is a huge muscle, a huge bearer, it could carry a person to America with ease, but not living. This is the strange marge of everything here. I would stay here only if I were a sea-bird or a creature like an otter, the dog of the sea, fit for these strands. The fit land of America is far. Sherkin my home is near, where the pollen flits, where each plant talks to the next with pollen, and the webs and the messages of lives run over the night lanes, and across fields under curious clouds. We are people for this place now right enough, we are caught in its purpose, a small manufactory that makes and unmakes, a bare stone cautiously marked with green life that is our blood and our dream.

Matt Purdy *shines out across the strand, he is yellow with light and has his heap of wings.*

Who art thou, my life?

Matt Purdy I am thy grand old man, Matt Purdy, an artisan of Manchester. This is our strand, yours and mine. I know you, the little fire that walks through the house, hearth of your father, the warm woman of my blood that is not afeared to walk out here where the wind bothers with no trifles and all is big and worse.

Fanny Thou art a first vision, Matt Purdy. Never have I seen thee before this.

Matt Purdy I am not a vision for thee, but out of my dead heart I bear for thee a kindly speech. It is something I must give thee, that I cannot give without this form. I did not live enough for thee. For I would give thee a lithographer out of Baltimore, a gentle man of little account who has borne his trouble. Moreover, I have given him a dream of thee, that he may come to fetch thee. For that he is a gentle heart. For Fanny, I would not have thee curious and alone here. Your heart beats up to me a message almost violent. Listen now, Fanny Hawke, and hear these calls.

Her name is called distantly by young voices. (Curlews, kittiwakes, gulls.)

Fanny Who is this calling me, Matt Purdy?

Matt Purdy They are the voices of thy children. They wait for you up the years, and you must go. All about them lies a cruel century of disasters and wars that I did not foresee. I steer you back into the mess of life because I was blinder than I knew. I saw a vision in time, that will not serve me outside time. I give you back to the coming century, Fanny, and your children are calling you. There are lives that are waiting to be made in a black century, and though they will see suffering, yet they will value their lives. Oh, in darkest heart they will cherish them. They can be nothing without Fanny Hawke. I, Matt Purdy, awkward artisan of the black city of Manchester, that fled from those streets of murder and loves too bleak to bear, give you a lithographer out of Baltimore to be thy husband and abide by thy side. Your children use the winds for their voices, (**Fanny** *raises a hand.*) and it is their happiness you must go to give. Hear this in place of my love that I could not give thee. I, Matt Purdy, battered angel, wanderer, simple founder, put you under promise of present love, that you may take your life from my words. I would kiss thee but that I am a tattered angel. Go, little

Fanny Hawke, into that Catholic darkness, into a century of
unlucky stars. So words in future time may be said of thee, that
thou did well to go, and said you would, and did, and rose
greatly to go.

Fanny *silent. A wide cloth of stars falls over* **Matt Purdy**.

John, *in mid channel, in the bow of* **Mr Moore**'s *rowing boat,* **Mr
Moore** *rowing strongly, both their faces twisted towards their destination
of Baltimore.* **John** *eager and drawn. The big Easter candle sticks up,
pointing forward,* **John**'s *arm guarding it. Gun-grey wind. They strive
forward.*

The bulk of the town in spring. **Patrick** *and* **Meg** *on the wharf, he
wrapped to the chin, she with a handsome coat gathered about her.*

Patrick There it is coming over now. Wouldn't you be hoarse
shouting for that boat? Give me a wish for a good journey,
though it's just a minute in a local boat.

Meg I won't say that it's not a good thing you are trying to do.

Patrick Give me your wish before it's tried, because after you
may not choose to speak to me.

Meg I? Not speak to the hero? I think I will speak to you.

Patrick Not in this town, I think – I hope she and I will be
March hares by then, or April, be deer by then, be wilder
creatures all wrapped and sitting up in a rough dogcart.

Meg I give you my wish, Patrick.

Patrick That's the whole matter that I needed. Thank you.

Meg Be careful, Patrick Kirwin, that you leave her a place to slumber, in the upshot.

Patrick I understand that. I intend to. Even if it's a long dry hedge of flowers stretched somewhere in the lost lands of this Ireland.

Meg A city bed will suit her. Here is my wish.

She touches his shoulder.

Patrick It's the smallest foolishest thing that holds the promise.

Mr Moore *brings in his boat.* **Patrick** *sees* **John** *struggling with the candle and he goes quickly to help. He draws it up.* **John** *climbs out.* **Patrick** *puts the candle in* **John***'s arms, nodding and smiling.* **John** *nodding and smiling.* **Meg** *gives him a slightly embarrassed wave of her hand.* **John** *heads up the town.* **Patrick** *into the boat.*

Patrick Am I all right for a crossing, sir?

Mr Moore (*looking after* **John**) You may be, if I lean in to these old oars.

The sweep of the bare sea. A sea music. A full burning light on the whitethorn, which is in first flower.

The room of the **Hawke** *house. Baskets gone, stove cold. Between the windows, a bowl of big spring flowers.* **Sarah** *and* **Hannah** *on their bench.* **Hannah** *biting off the last thread on new backing to an old dark dress. She pushes it up on the back of the bench, where it lies stiffly, like a third person almost. She has a folded cloth on her lap, which she shakes out and spreads on their knees.* **Sarah** *feels it.*

Sarah What have I stitched here with you, Hannah?

Hannah Why, Sarah, none. It is a clear cloth. A clear.

Sarah (*laughing*) Are you certain? I feel some little workings here.

Hannah That's the little snags. Gatherings of the weaver. It will make an adequate bed cloth. But best cloth would be the wrong praise for it.

Sarah (*touching her head*) There is sun on my crown.

Hannah It is a perfect freshened spring morning. I will go and bring joy to that pig's stomach in a moment. That present three-day soup has reached its fifth day. Into our pig it must go. It is very wicked of us to be stitching at this hour, but the light is better for you.

Sarah Oh, yes. Far better. Thank you, dear.

Patrick, *his arms full of flowers, steps in carefully.*

(*Staring over, sniffing.*) Who is this person with the spring?

Hannah *is flustered to see a stranger.*

Patrick How do you do, ma'am? I am looking for Miss Fanny Hawke. My name is Patrick Kirwin, ma'am. From the town there, over.

Sarah (*to* **Hannah**, *frightened*) Who is this man?

Hannah *looks at* **Patrick**, *trying to know him.*

Hannah (*at last*) How did you get out here so early, Mr, Mr – ?

Patrick I shouted across to a figure on the pier. I shouted my poor head away. And Mr Moore came over and got me.

Hannah What a wonderful pair of ears Moore has.

Patrick It was terribly still. It is golden water there this morning, but glass-clear. A better man than me might have just walked across.

Sarah (*to* **Hannah**) Was that a low remark?

Patrick He had a big, dark-suited sort of a fellow in the boat with him, that carried a great giant of a candle, so I suppose he was heading over anyway.

Hannah Fanny is out there somewhere searching for our hens' eggs.

Sarah (*in a friendly fashion, finally*) You never had hens like ours. They would lay in your ear and not tell you. You could search for a week, and be deaf the whole time. You have never had mad hens, sir?

Patrick I have met a few. In people's yards, you know.

Hannah Go out to her loudly. Do not make her jump by creeping about. Although it is unlikely, she may have just a few eggs in her dress, and we would rather you did not cause her to break them.

Patrick *nods. Goes away out.*

Half the island's flowers in his arms, that man had. (*Shakes her head.*)

Sarah Heh, Hannah, do you think our little hens would ever reach heaven?

Hannah They get in everywhere else. Why not heaven too?

Patrick, *awkwardly, in the area of the whitethorn. He is cold, with his flowers. He sees the sheltered place in against the whitethorn and sits there, still holding the flowers. He grows comfortable, sleepy, topples slightly, wakes, stirs himself a little, but sleeps again. After a short while,* **Fanny** *appears, holding a front pocket lightly, where she has stored a few eggs. She pokes about in places that she knows, with no luck. She gets to the other side of the whitethorn, carefully rolling up the sleeve of one arm, and reaches in amid the scrubby grass, and with some triumph finds two eggs, which she happily looks at, one in each palm. She hears a slight snore, steps around the whitethorn. She takes him in.*

Fanny Oh. The loved one.

Patrick *wakes. He jumps in half-sleep, sees her, tries to get up, is hampered by the flowers, but he makes it,* **Fanny** *stepping back to give him room. She is still holding out the eggs.* **Patrick** *grips the flowers tightly.*

Patrick My speech, my speech. (*As if by rote*.) I did spend such a winter. (**Fanny** *silent*.) That's to say, a happy one. A happy winter. A change of things. The house was different. (*Differently*.) You know why I've come out here? (**Fanny** *nods*.) Since you know. (*Abruptly*.) I dreamt of something. (*Workmanlike*.) I've purchased a new premises in Cork City, it is beside the new theatre hall. If you don't mind comedians and risky dancers too much, we might stick our sign beside such light and splendour.

Fanny (*in wonder*) The theatre hall?

Patrick Over the shop are two entire floors, for a house of children. A spring-cleaning. A new start. Well. Dear Lord.

Fanny *gathers words to speak, opens her mouth, but only gabbles.*

Is this the desert of the world, this island? No. I did try to get away, I went away from Baltimore, you see, but you see, I brought you with me, you know, in the noggin. It was just like having the sun on my head all winter. Heh. (*He smiles*.) My friend, if you will, you will come with me to Cork City.

She makes her leap of faith.

Fanny (*finding her words*) Go yourself to Baltimore now, Patrick. Wait there a last while. I will come to you before dark.

Patrick There's no doubt? You'll deliver yourself from your place?

Fanny Yes. I will go from my family like a dreamer, and wake in the new world.

Patrick It's my joy.

Fanny It is mine. (*Putting the eggs quickly and carefully into her pocket with the others*.) Let me touch your face. (*She does*.) Go on away out.

He goes, still clutching the flowers. **Fanny** *remains a moment, holding the pocket of eggs gently, she heads slowly towards the house.*

*The **Hawke** house. **Hannah** cleans the shell-toy with flicks of a duster of goose feathers. **Sarah** by the bench, holding the mended dress to herself, gauging it.*

Sarah Will that fellow take some three-day soup, do you think?

Hannah (*looking out of window, watching **Patrick** go by*) I think he will take no three-day soup here.

Sarah Well, he will not get soup like mine in his own place.

Hannah A creature like that has no place, maybe.

Sarah There is a leaf on this island that does something to soup.

Hannah Wild mint. It is miraculous soup. It is plain soup.

Fanny *comes in. Stops, seems to think about speaking. Goes on through to the kitchen, past **Sarah**. **Hannah** follows slowly to the door.*

Sarah Is that the child? I smelled eggs.

Hannah How can you smell eggs, Sarah?

*She looks in at **Fanny**.*

Sarah I do not know. I hope I cannot smell the rear end of a hen now. I would not care for that.

Hannah (*to **Fanny***) You found a few handy?

No answer.

Patrick *alone. He throws the flowers from him, they spread about. He brushes off stray blossoms. **Jesse** approaches, with a long twig.*

Jesse (*very friendly*) What is this mysterious custom, (*Meaning the flowers.*) Patrick Kirwin?

Patrick Ah, Jesse. (*Acknowledging flowers.*) Ah, they weren't needed in the upshot. How's Jesse, anyway?

Jesse Jesse? (*Puts the twig in his teeth.*) Nesting, nesting!

Patrick Why wouldn't you, Jess, (*Patting his shoulder briefly.*) why wouldn't you?

Jesse You have been a while away from us.

Patrick I was in the city. There was a host of things there you'd care for. I saw a mariner's telescope, but to be honest, there was a terrible price on it. I suppose it's the brass in it, Jesse. Look now, I'll be away. Are you fine? (*Moves away. Comes back to shake* **Jesse**'s *hand vigorously.*)

The **Hawke** *house.* **Sarah**'s *black dress on the bench, light glimmering along it.* **Fanny** *just inside the room,* **Hannah** *by her.* **Sarah** *close by.* **Fanny** *bewildered.*

Hannah A marriage? A marriage?

Jesse *comes in*

A going-away, Fanny?

Hannah *cries.*

Is that Father back from Baltimore, Jesse?

Jesse Oh, yes. Just in. I did see him, mid-channel, from the yellow hill.

Hannah Please do run for him, Jesse, please do run.

Jesse *turns and runs through switches and twigs of light to* **John**, *in his workroom unpacking a new store of nuns' wax.*

John No piece of something for us, child?

Jesse, *panting, thinks, looks in his trouser pockets.*

Jesse No bread. No bread. There is someone come. (*Holding* **John**'s *sleeve.*) He said there is only the one quarry in the whole world. One, Father!

John Who is come?

Jesse *knocks his knuckles on his head.*

Is it someone then maybe from Manchester?

Jesse No, no, a man that was tired of murders. He is Fanny's own man.

John (*knowing who it must be*) Do you see this for wax? The nuns were besotted with that lovely big candle. I will never get over the enthusiasm of nuns. (*Differently.*) And is he still on Sherkin, your man, Jesse?

Jesse He is not my man. It is Fanny's man. (*Suddenly.*) I hope I did not cause it!

John Jesse. (*Holding his shoulders.*) My excellent son. You are a scientific person. I know the man, and the history, and have spoken with Fanny. Beloved boy.

Jesse I ran like a rabbit, Father. I have forgot the bread to revive you. I have given you this news as fast as I was able.

John My sweet son. We will go and see. (*Touching the wax.*) A work is enough to hold our world.

The **Hawke** *house,* **Fanny,** **Hannah** *and* **Sarah** *barely moved.* **Jesse** *and* **John** *come in,* **John** *stays at the door. He looks at* **Fanny,** *knows.* **Fanny** *returns his look. He sinks his head a little.*

Towards twilight, slow deepening of light. A simple music. The table is set with their dishes, **John**, **Jesse** *and* **Fanny** *in their places.* **Hannah** *comes in from kitchen with a bowl of food, sits. They wait for* **Sarah**. **John** *looks at* **Hannah**. **Sarah** *comes in with lighted taper. A gust of early evening wind comes in the windows, makes the shell-toy murmur, and blows out* **Sarah**'s *taper. She doesn't realise it. She locates the candle on the windowsill by her, feels the wick, thinks she is lighting it.*

Hannah Do not bother with the candles now, Sarah.

Hannah *lets her go on to the other candles. After 'lighting' the candles on the table,* **Sarah** *'blows out' the taper.*

Sarah (*standing near* **Fanny**, *the taper crossed on her hands*) When I was a girl with Charity, we walked often on the strand beyond the last dunes, where the tide ticks, does it not? And sometimes we were shocked by freshwater ducks that stood out there maybe resting between flying. How little envy we had for those ducks, stout creatures though they were, since we were bright in the fold of the families. And those small shells, that we could see through to the great sky with, she used to strew about, and she said they were like fingernails, that any Hawke or Smith or Purdy had on their fingers, that showed they were of Sherkin. And she said, all those years after, that I wasn't to let her go off Sherkin without a handful of those shells somewhere put in with her, and I did that, yes.

Sarah *crosses to the door leading outside.*

Hannah Where are you heading now, Sarah, dear? Our meal is here for us.

Sarah I have no need of the meal just now.

She goes to step out.

Hannah You cannot go walking about out there now, Sarah. It will be quite dark in just a little.

Sarah I am afraid it is of no import to me now, the failing light.

She goes out.

(*Off.*) On this island anyhow I need nothing so extravagant as eyes.

Hannah (*getting up*) I am not that ready for eating now, myself. I will go up to the cupboards with myself.

She goes out by kitchen.

John You can walk around this island in a fifth of a day. You may see the part ruined by the great force of the Atlantic, and by the channel sheltered you may see the hopeful farms. The strand is peaceful this evening, but the Atlantic is broiling far out. Nothing breaks the wild surface of the storm there but dolphins and angels.

Fanny *looks at him.*

Jesse Do you go easily? You do not at all. You go like our father's dolphins, breaking into the stormy air. You will need all your muscles.

Fanny *smiles at him.*

John (*arranged for his prayer*) If you do please, Lord, this is our night prayer. We do ask you for the peace of this family. We do ask you for the silence and the storm of Sherkin. Once there were three families, Lord, that – (*He looks forward, shakes his head, in difficulties.*)

Hannah *comes back, carrying an old wooden case.* **Fanny** *stands up.*

Hannah This is one of the old Manchester cases, can you credit that? You would think the worms would have long devoured it. But there are still four of them above on the byre rafters. Look at this label. There is a picture of a sailing ship, but I cannot read the names. This is your proper hope-chest, Fanny, with tansy and heart's-ease to freshen the clothes.

Fanny I do thank thee.

Hannah (*at the label again*) It must say the name of the ship. It must give the place of destination. Is it not a queer old case?

They called this a sea box, the old women. (*Patting her chest, pointing at herself.*) The old women! Think of the women of this house. I gather them all together in my mind, as no doubt they will gather on the splendid day. Why, we will abide and there will be the day when all the women of this house rise up from the yard and we will have a holiday rowing them with honeysuckle to the twelve gates. Oh, I do not doubt it. See, (*Opening the lid of the case.*) see under there, what I have slipped in for you.

Fanny *comes closer to see. She lifts out a framed mirror, looks in puzzlement at* **Hannah.**

Now, child, whose mirror is that, would you say? (*Laughing.*) Oh, child, child, do you think no one ever owned a mirror? There is not such a terrible strictness on every side. The river of light flows despite many a curiosity. That is your mother's mirror, Charity's mirror, and it is a plain thing enough for a vade-mecum. (*Puts her hands over* **Fanny**'s *holding the mirror.*) We will hold gently.

Fanny Will you kiss me?

Hannah *kisses her. They refasten the case.*

Hannah I have forgotten your coat and bonnet.

Hannah *goes again to fetch them.* **John** *gets up, comes round to* **Fanny.**

John When you were born I was out in the first field digging, and I dug the better because you were nearing. I pleased myself to watch a flight of land-birds going away over to America and having no cognisance of my luck. Sarah Purdy was standing in the frame of that window. She flung up the casement and called out to me to run in. I burst through this room and flew up the stairs. Charity was a thing of sweat, and our bed was a wild splash of blood and matter. Out of our human earth had risen a strange red-skinned girl, that Hannah held fast in her arms, and poor Sarah was still calling at the window, as if I had not heard, though I had run right past her. Why, I kissed my Charity and my bawling child, and sick with joy, walked out onto the bare strands. There was a singing in the wind all full of your name,

Fanny Hawke, Fanny Hawke, and I that never could dance
could dance that day, and I danced, and shook out my legs.
(*After a moment.*) Remember these things, Fanny.

He embraces her.

Fanny I will, Father. I will remember everything.

John Child, I love thee.

Hannah *back with the coat and bonnet. Helps her with it.* **Fanny** *is
ready to go. She stops by* **Jesse** *and with her free hand touches his cheek.*

Fanny Goodbye, little brother, with your long face.

Outside, **Sarah** *in the yard. She has sand on her shoes and her lower skirts
are damp. She has small shells in one hand, she is making them grind
lightly against each other. It is quite twilight now.*

Fanny Sarah. You are nearly home again.

Sarah Oh, I am relieved, Fanny, I thought I might have taken
the wrong path and be among the yard of the hotel buildings.

Fanny No, you are by me here. You need walk only a few steps
further. Our house is near.

Sarah (*gripping* **Fanny**'s *hands, giving her shells*) Hannah says I
have a cold hand, for a bed companion. Do I have a cold hand,
Fanny?

Fanny Yes.

Sarah Here is a little question, for I see, or imagine, that you are
going. If I wished it to go with you, would you take me, with
even these eyes?

Fanny Oh yes, come if you wish. I wish it. I will buy you such
spectacles.

Sarah No. That is all that I wished. I can stay here easier if I know you would have taken me. I am for this place mostly, I think, Fanny.

Fanny Let me take you back into the house, Sarah, dear.

Sarah No. This is my path here. (*Going purposefully forward.*) Now I will go along it. (*Turning to her.*) May thy own journey be as safe and bright, my love.

Fanny *walks between the darkening hedges.*

The pier. **Eoghan**'s *currach. He is readying to row out home. He has lit a lamp, that is fixed on a pole at the bow. It is a candle in a square glass. It sheds its light on the water.* **Fanny** *with her sea-box.*

Fanny Fisherman?

Eoghan (*surprised*) Yes?

Fanny Fisherman, will you take me over?

Eoghan In this falling dark?

Fanny Yes.

Eoghan To Baltimore?

Fanny Yes. Will you take me across?

Eoghan I will, I will take you.

Out on the water. **Fanny** *in the stern seat, her sea-box held firmly.* **Eoghan** *rows. The darkening sea spreads all around. Plash of oars in still air. The lamp shedding light. A quiet moon, above. In his own bright light,* **John** *comes to the end of the pier.* **Eoghan** *rows,* **John**'s *light diminishes plash by plash. He can barely see his daughter. He gives a* *slight wave to her. His light extinguishes. Slowly, the other side, from the darkest shadow, on the wharf at Baltimore, light grows on* **Patrick**, *looking out, worriedly waiting. Plash by plash his light increases.*

Curtain.

Boss Grady's Boys

To Philip Casey

Boss Grady's Boys was first performed at the Abbey Theatre (Peacock stage), Dublin, on 22 August 1988 with the following cast:

Mick	Jim Norton
Josey	Eamon Kelly
Mrs Molloy	Maureen Toal
Mrs Swift	Máire O'Neill
Mr Reagan	Gerard McSorley
Father	Oliver Maguire
Mother	Bríd Ní Neachtain
Girl	Gina Moxley

Directed by Caroline FitzGerald
Designed by Carol Betera
Lighting by Tony Wakefield
Music by Thomas McLaughlin

Characters

Mick, *sixties, small, slight. Hair still dark.*
Josey, *seventies, larger than his brother* **Mick**, *sandy-white hair.*
Mrs Molloy, *sixties, ample.*
Mrs Swift, *sixties, grey, trim.*
Mr Reagan, *sixties, meagre.*
Father, *Boss Grady, medium height, stocky, bellied, in his sixties. Father of* **Mick** *and* **Josey**.
Mother, *late twenties, tallish, scraggy, long thin reddish face.*
Girl, *eighteen, small, undernourished, unappealing, thin hair, almost bald.*

The play is set on a forty-acre hill-farm on the Cork/Kerry border.

Note on the first production

In the first production, the stage was arranged differently than printed here. The fireplace was a solid affair, and was positioned extreme right. The two windows in the text became one good-sized window upstage centre, on the ledge of which Josey had his 'kitchen'; there was a niche here also for the fiddle, which allowed Josey to use it in the final moments of Act Two, playfully, as a gun; the window was attached to the stairs, going up a little way to nowhere. The scenes, marked in the text by gaps, were connected during rehearsals by movements that fitted the existing dialogue; there were few blackouts as a result. Also the window, stairs and fireplace were on stage from the start, and everything took place as it were in the house. In Act Two, page 119, the threshold was considered as downstage centre, and the horse crossing was indicated by sound only.

In Act One, page 94, the bed remained on stage, and was used for a horse, instead of one suggested by light. The dancers did not appear in Act Two, page 106.

Sebastian Barry
Dublin, 1989

Act One

Curtain.

Mick *sitting on the ground, slightly to left of centre, with a large purple sweep of light as of a mountain beyond him. He is a smallish figure, with a fishing hat on his head. He has his back to us, with his legs gripped in. It is evening, but early, and there is a full rich red in the sky above the mountain, which burns. The sky deepens and sweeps from right to left in a hurry. As a wind blows against his back he grips closer, keeping his head low, but watching the sunset. All around him is shadowy. The sky as it loses the sun gets deeper and deeper red, till it goes out. Then* **Mick** *is left in a dark blue light obscuring the stage.*

A tiny glimmer of light appears where the sun went and this increases to the dull glow of a turf fire. **Mick** *is in the same spot, but turned three-quarters to us, on a stool, staring into the fire. He is wearing the same black working trousers, an old nylon shirt, but without his hat. His face is hard and neat, shaven, his hair blackish, trained back, cropped close.*

Josey *comes into the light from the other side, the right, pulling up a backed kitchen chair.* **Josey**'s *hair is sandy-white, wavy but thinnish, a little too long. He wears brown working trousers, a whitish shirt, and a brown jacket. He has his cap in his hand, which he then settles on his head. He sits in his place, the fire between them.*

Josey I'd make tea for a halfpenny. Will I bring the horse down and put him closer to the house? I don't like the creature up there above the house in this rain.

Mick *stares with his own thoughts into the fire.*

Josey I was thinking today all day there was likely to be a deal of rain later, and now it has held off till night-time. There's something in the weather that it's always the same. You can predict it after a fashion. Well, Mick? So.

Mick (*not looking at him*) There's just wind.

Josey Is there no rain? Then the horse can talk to himself in peace. Will I call in the old dog so?

Mick (*looking up at him*) You old bastard. Can you not enjoy the fire?

Josey The old dog will be cold. He has no good bones left. Every one of them is a nuisance to him. But he is a very lovable dog.

Mick We've no dog now, Josey man. You buried him. He's up to his neck in soil, and I'm sorry for it. The sheep knew him well. It will trouble me to train a new one.

Josey It was lovely how he lay in the grass with the sheep. He was such a big mess of black. The sheep loved him.

Mick You fool. The sheep loved him? He never did lay down with the sheep.

Josey No, Mick. I meant when you were steering them. I meant when you told him to go down, when you had them going right. Just how he dropped down, the big black fellow. Collapsed at your word. You see I enjoyed that. The sheep loved him.

Mick The sheep didn't love him.

Josey Well. He was very black and he lay in the grass. In the summer he looked well enough in the grass, when the grass was drier. Will I shout from the door for him?

Mick Christ, man.

Josey You have great whistles.

Josey *stands, sticks his hands in his pockets, leans forwards. He gives a weak whistle, waves an arm. He gives two whistles, and laughs, and tries to whistle, calms, waves an arm.*

Mick Quiet yourself.

Josey I'm driving the sheep into the slope field, because the grass there is perfect, perfect. Listen to me.

Josey *whistles again, and calls.*

Shep! Shep! Shep! Gubb-a-bubb-em! Down, down!

He is nearly weeping.

Mick Ah, man. You've just driven the sheep away up across the hill. The dog's died from contradiction.

Josey (*laughing*) Bloody me! Aye, aye, aye.

He twirls himself, and makes a dance gesture, spreading out his hands, one foot out to the side, and holds it, and attempts a tap dance.

Mick You're feeling your oats.

Josey I am, heart. I am. Fred Astaire, man. I'm a great dancer. There will be a lady in a satin dress in here, if you don't stop me.

Mick (*savagely*) Sit down and shut up.

Josey *chastened, settles his cap, and sits again. They both stare at the fire.*

The same, but the fire is just a low ashen glow.

Josey (*leaning in*) We would never go to Killarney now for the pictures, I suppose. Groucho Marx is a great man. The head of the country that time. (*Sings.*) Hail Freedonia! Hail Freedonia! (*From the song in the Marx Brothers'* Duck Soup.) It was a lovely song. I loved the ducks in the pot, with the steam, but the ducks were all right. And that lovely woman with the big soft bosom. A soft night. A woman of a sort you won't see often in Bantry, unless she's a foreign woman staying in the big hotel. I would choose to marry ten women like that, and have them all in the loft stacked like big hayricks. We could lie on them and pray for help. The Yankee horses would come streaming up the track, with a pretty clatter, and rescue us.

Mick (*affectionately*) You old fool, you.

Josey Groucho, Harpo, Chico, and what's-his-name, and what was the name of the Frenchy man, the singer, on the boat with them that time?

Mick You old blasted fool.

Josey He was old in that picture, old but handsome, the perfect man for the bosomy lady.

Mick You know, I remember his name. It was Maurice Chevalier.

Josey What was his name, what was his name?

Mick *looks at him, blinks slowly.*

Josey It's like wringing the necks of hens.

Mick *is standing on a small wooden stairs, downstage right, shadowed. He is looking at* **Josey** *who is hunched over the embers of the fire.* **Josey** *has his hands outstretched to embrace the heat. There is a noise of waterdrops hissing in the embers.*

Josey The rain now. Coming in the same as October's rats from the cold. The horse will be a lonely man in the field. There'll be mud now on his hooves, and he has no fire or talk to protect him. Maybe I should have walked up in the cold and got him. He could stand outside the door here and listen to us. He could do so. It was like when Mick Collins was all the fashion, and Mick was away every night, and then every night away after that, when the old man was dead as a dog and the farm was ours in a way. It was our farm and no one came up the track to say otherwise. There were hens galore with brown eggs in them, there were two old pigs that wouldn't breed any more, there were more sheep, and a milking cow to boot. It is like that now, as if Mick were away all night at his game, and the country very silent in its manner around me. It is like that, with a bat coming in from the dark and losing his way in the firelight. Mick away, and the dark roof moving with the firelight. Mick away. Little heat from the fire in this state, the moon in her own house, Collins the same man that was buried afterwards. He was a big black man with a greasy face. Mick told me. He was the king of the country in his time. He was a lonely sort of man, I suppose. And he made me lonely. I'd make tea for a halfpenny.

Mick Josey, come to bed.

A marriage bed to the left, one side facing us. **Mick** *is lying on it on his side, with his face towards us, eyes open.* **Josey** *is vaguer behind him, his face turned up to the ceiling can be seen. They are covered in worn army blankets with a faded coverlet on top. The sheets are flannelette, brownish, the pillow is the one bolster.* **Mick** *has a finger in his mouth. There is a bit of a candle lighting his face, but the space beside the end of the bed, which is ample, is empty and pitch.* **Mick**'s *expression responds slightly to what* **Josey** *says.*

Josey A little bit of everything. A little bit of woe, a bit of mirth. A bit of bread, a bit of good butter. (*After a bit.*) Bless you, and bless us in return. Bless this small house and bless me and Mick. Bless the sheep and the dog and the horse. Go up and talk to the horse in his field in your overcoat. Bless the piece of money in the bank in Killarney, if it's still there.

Mick *throws his eyes quickly.*

Bless the trees and the whins, and the rowanberries and the berries on them. Bless the rain and the rare sun and the seasons four. Bless the mam in heaven and the length of time since we seen her. Bless the gate and the slope field, and the rocky land at the top of the farm, which is no good to us. Bless our jackets and the few trousers and the shoes and the leather laces Mick bought this year. Bless the potatoes and the swedes and keep them whole and hale in their pit when the time comes to bury them in. That will be October. Bless the dog.

He pauses. **Mick** *stares, waiting.*

Bless. Bless. Bless. Bless the old man. Bless the turf. Bountiful Mary, come into us this night and bless us. Take your old blue cloak off for us, and God bless you, and bless the cups and the spoons, and bless the old fiddle ruined with damp, that the old man cherished as his own bride, and that is propped in the niche of the window. Bless the postman should he come, and bless the Bantry road, both to the town and to the mountains. Good night to you.

Mick *wets his fingers and snuffs the candle.*

Josey Bless the darkness, come to that.

Mick's *dream.*

The bed very dimly seen, with two masks in place of the two men's faces. To the right of this, in the clear space, is a table with four people playing cards. An oil-lamp behind them gives light. This, starting from nothing, is becoming brighter as the figures animate, then the scene darkens again. After a second or two the scene returns with the lamp fully lit, and exactly as the light is established, one of the two widows speaks. These are the widows of shopkeepers in Bantry. The other man is a widower, a shopkeeper himself.

Mrs Molloy What is it about cards that makes you thirsty? Is it the excitement?

She means this sarcastically. They are playing poker. **Mrs Swift** *can not make up her mind.*

Mrs Swift Hold up a minute, dear. Just let a girl think. There's a cabinet of alcohol behind you, if you want it.

Mrs Molloy I wouldn't dream, I wouldn't dream.

Mrs Swift You don't want me to get it for you?

Mrs Molloy Would you stop, and ask Mr Reagan for your cards. You're making a very long job of it.

Mr Reagan Two or three?

Mrs Swift I don't know. What do you think?

Mr Reagan Don't show me! This is a game for profit, Mrs Swift. Have a heart.

Mrs Molloy Mr Grady?

Mick (*surprised in his thoughts*) No.

Mrs Molloy What do you mean, no?

Mick Were you not asking me if I wanted a drink?

Mrs Molloy Man, you are worse than she is.

Mrs Swift There's whiskey behind you all in the cabinet. Dear me – two cards, please, Mr Reagan.

Mick I'll have the four. I can do nothing with these.

Mrs Molloy Keep your cards close to your chest, Mr Grady, and a poker face. I hope you have that ace.

Mick I need an ace?

Mrs Molloy To get four cards again you do.

Mick Well, I have it of course. (*Pleasantly.*) Do you want to examine it?

Mrs Molloy Examine it? Keep it to yourself. I am indifferent to it.

Mick What sort of whiskey, Mrs Swift? Irish?

Mrs Swift Not at all. Good Scotch.

Mick As I feared, as I feared.

Mrs Molloy (*standing*) As I feared, as I feared. A life of romance was the least a girl should expect. It was a good life in a way, but his shop was a mean shop, and there were too many items from

India. He took away every year I had to give a man, and then took away himself for good measure. He was a man after my own heart so I will not blame him. (*Sitting.*) This is a tedious game after a while. It is not really a lady's game.

Mr Reagan What is a lady's game in effect? Bridge?

Mrs Molloy That is a fine lady's game. But I can not play it.

Mrs Swift It needs brains. I can't play it either. It's a rich person's game.

Mrs Molloy There is often something very feeble and silly about you, Mrs Swift.

Mrs Swift Did you want that drink now, Mrs Molloy? I realise you want one.

Mrs Molloy (*standing, to herself*) I wanted one, I did want one. Curly things the same as bees. I think woods are glad of bees, the babies of woods. I wanted a little son I could watch all his first years, and hear talk, and he could have gone to school and come home, simply, richly. I wanted a head to stroke, a head of hair, black hair. There is something about a boy of nine that is preferable to a girl. He looks at the world with innocence, but is a creature to take his place in it all the same, a king. Whereas, alas, as I know myself, the life of a girl is just the dickens. Every man in the street will touch you or look at you, and in the lanes among the bread-and-cheese bushes, when the May is on the branches, and the bees idle like engines, and the big cars ease through the mid-morning, someone will come thrashing through the nettles and the docks over the ditch, and drag you into a quiet glade and yank up your skirt and murder his joke into you. A girl of nine should not go out walking in an Irish lane, when the May is out. (*Sits.*)

Mick Are you going to give me four, Eamon?

Mr Reagan Are you innocent of them? Sorry. (*He gives* **Mick** *four new cards.*) A bit of butter, a bit of bread. Fresh from Killarney. Comes in at six, you know, around the new coast road. We call it the new road because heretofore we were not in contact with the

mainland, as we dubbed it, though we are not an island. My
wife, usually a well woman, is buried some while since. We sell
the *Press*, the *Independent* and the *Examiner*, but not the *Irish Times*.
Though this is a planter town, which you might not expect so far
south, we don't stock the *Irish Times* as a rule. There is very little
reading in it, unless you are a Dublin man, or gentry. There are
no gentry in this district, nor has been for many a long decade.
We got rid of them quite. We burned them out. They were glad
to leave and, indeed, we have baking powder, and custard, and
even oats if you wanted them for your porridge. Every brand
name you can think of lives in here a merry merry life.

Mrs Swift I have a right bellyache from that chicken. What can
Dempsey's be thinking of, stocking chicken as tough as boots? I
had to boil it for two days. Which included two nights. I heard it
in the pantry, bubbling away in the heart of the old house. How
very pretty my rooms look in the sunlight, in the night-time I
often think they are a little tomblike, a little less than decent. My
missal however keeps me going. There are some lovely prayers in
the missal. Don't you often think that, Mrs Molloy? But I doubt
if you would, with your roly-poly body and happy air and
attraction to men. But if you asked my opinion, in a month of
Sundays, your face is the visage of a horse, with a touch of hair
where hair ought not to be on a woman. But never mind, have
another piece of gâteau. This is fresh gâteau from Killarney and
Mr Reagan's shopeen. It looks like the flesh of an old man's
belly, my nice old man who never laid a hand on me without his
mass-gloves on. I can not abide, or could not in the days when
Declan was still living, the touch of a living man's hand on my
person. It gave me the chills, such as was not to be
countenanced. And yet, in the happy cinema in Killarney years
ago, it was a different matter were a youth such as, well, whoever
he might be, to just for a moment, just for a moment, well, fondle
me. (*Clearing her throat.*) I wouldn't be seen dead in the street
without my foundation and face-powder, though I understand
from the younger set that powder has gone out of fashion. I like
the puff and the case in my handbag always. I suppose they
don't wear stays either. But some people are ill-advised not to

wear stays. The trees in the little square stay firm even in old age, but we, well, really, it's obvious.

Mick I've nothing.

Mrs Molloy Everything comes to him who waits. Don't be a girl ever in a boy's world. Last winter I went out in the yard with a pan of cinders and threw them glowing on the snow.

Mr Reagan Are we playing cards or what? I don't mean to pry. Tomorrow I may go out from the town for good and become a countryman proper. Set up on a hill farm like Mick and his brother, and be simple. I can then be in a position to walk to the town from the farm and back again, through light rain, and will be especially excited by the numerous murmurings of small chaffinches and robins and sparrows. A light fiddle-music, giving rise to the traditional music. I'd rather be done with it here than endure another odd night above in Crow Street in my little room.

Mrs Swift Well, come to that, I might put on every inch of good stuff I have, and go out on the Killarney road and be taken in by some traveller – commercial but not tinker. It really is a bonus not having to submit to gentle entreaties. I much prefer the greatness of our air, the famous Irish air that the foreigners love. I am glad we can be so giving to the foreigners, with our air. The foreigners are very fine people, very fine. They came from all over.

Mick We appear to be stuck with this hand. Will we play something else?

Mrs Molloy (*standing, putting her leg up on the table, showing a garter*) We could play house. That's a good game.

Mick It's not a card game though, you know.

Mrs Molloy There's something I've always liked about you, Mick Grady. You may be a small wizened little creature with a square face and dark skin denoting I don't know what, but you have an advantage, a steal on other men in these parts. I am a

very soft person, you know, that might be sunk into, with profit.
(*She sits.*)

Mick Rightyo, rightyo. Time to go home. Time to go home.
Josey will still be up.

Mr Reagan How is your brother, Mick? Is he in good fettle?

Mick He is. But he is also a man that feels loneliness very
keenly, and begins to pine if I'm away long. He forgets to make
tea for himself, or cannot do it if I am not at home. He is a very
peculiar, unnecessary brother that I have come to revere and
value by hook and by crook.

Mr Reagan Is your brother well, Mick?

Mick My brother is a well, deep, stony and dry. I throw stones
into the poor man that echo with a lost, deep sort of echo. I love
him, I love his idiocy.

Mick *turns about, and kneels on his chair, turned from the others, facing
upstage left. Two high columns of variously coloured light like stained-
glass windows appear, strengthen, displacing the other scene. Light falls
through the windows onto* **Mick.**

Mick Lord of the streams, the hills, the farms, of the farmers,
what's wrong with us, what's amiss with us? I'm a smallish man.
I would like a slightly larger acreage, with a deal of sunlight to
improve the grazing. I don't actually. (*To himself.*) I won't talk to
glass windows any more. I won't go along with them. Let the old
women do it. Old bastes, old cattle, I won't have a word for
them any more. It's idle little, idle little. On my knees in front of
windows. On my knees as if He was an English lord. If He met
me on the road in his car He would spit through the side window
at me. Long ago in his pony-and-trap He would have leant out
with His whip, and stroked me with it. Down on my knees.

He stretches out his arms.

Away up the road with you, you foreigner you!

Windows disappear, lamplight returns, **Mick** *sits as before.*

Mr Reagan We never see your brother in the town now. Is he well? We went to the same school and we never see him now. He was a great fellow for catching wrens. He had the knack. He could catch a wren nimbly with lime on a stick and he might weep for it after, but what can you do?

Mick With all my red heart I wish he might not survive me alone in the house. And yet I wish that I might not survive him. I will not live here with his shadow and our father's shadow, and I expect I will. They would certainly not leave him be, if they ever saw him do what I see him do. He is a brother that many people would be glad to know. A diverse brother but a comfortable one. He would never get in your way willingly or knowingly.

Mrs Molloy I suppose people say odd things about me. I am bothered by the thought. I always like to be liked where possible. Of course I am a dryish woman, an empty sort. There was a deal of love in me at one time. Someone to caress me.

Mick Well, there's my hand. (*Putting down the cards.*)

Mr Reagan Is there no more betting? I suppose not if you've shown. You have three kings and a pair of tens. That's enough to lick me.

Mrs Swift I had only a number of very different cards. I've no luck tonight.

Mr Reagan There's no real need to say what you had if you don't wish, I believe.

Mrs Swift I don't mind telling you. I wanted to. All through the game I felt a little foolish, holding such cards, and betting pennies on them.

Mrs Molloy (*looking at her, almost kindly*) You ought to have stopped, Mrs Swift. Don't you know you can stop?

Mrs Swift Of course.

Lamp fades.

Josey's *dream.*

The bed, as before. In the clear space on the right it is blueish, misty, with a sparkling of light from the ground to the extreme right, where the water is. A middle-sized, thick-set man with wavy white hair, in his sixties, dressed in workclothes, comes carefully from the left carrying a fishing-rod and a bundle of line whose hooks have cork stuck on the tips, a round float at the end. It is stormy.

Father It has to be a storm inside a mist.

Josey (*offstage left*) Dad! Have I lost my way? Am I right for the lake?

Father A curious thing that the storm takes his words and carries them to me. (*He puts down the line at the water's edge and arranges and then casts his fly-rod.*) If I catch a trout in this wind I will know a great deal. But it has to be a storm inside a mist.

Josey (*coming on muddily*) I never trust that path.

Father There is no path that I know of.

Josey I've crossed it a few times and I don't still believe it will take me.

Father (*nodding at the lake*) What do you think?

Josey There are crazy fish in there today.

Father They'd always be in there, Josey. It's a lake.

Josey Well, I can smell them, I can smell them!

Father Then you have a fine nose. I have only mist in mine. It's funny that we came up here, the only lake in Cork or Kerry that needs a storm, in a place that has no road after the mountain road, and where the trout are the wiliest buggers alive. You need to be a genius to catch these trout, and in a storm at that.

Josey The storm makes them hungry.

Father I expect so. It is called Hungry Hill.

Josey There are many big trout under the waves today, Dad. Are we to throw out the line?

Father If we catch one on the rod, we'll throw the line out. We'll try the line if we catch one now. (*Working the rod.*)

Josey There is something fierce about the fish up here. Isn't there a very wicked look to them, to their jaws? Do you remember when you brought me up here with the other men, and you made a line with fifty hooks, and stood both sides of the lake and walked its length? And you got as many as thirty fish, each one bigger and wickeder than the last.

Father I don't. I don't remember.

Josey There was a blue colour at the top of the sky, a strange blue colour like it was hot, and the fog was clothy and bright, and the edges of the grass tufts gleamed at the light. You and the men shouted across the water to each other, and it was a very bright storm with lights. It was very exciting.

Father No. I don't recall that.

Josey I was very young at the time. Perhaps that is why. It is hard to remember when you are very young.

Father There are no fish in here today I think.

Josey There must be. Fish away.

Father No, there are none. It's not likely you'll get one if you don't get one straight away.

Josey It is such a long walk. Fish away.

Father No, it will be better if we go down. We're wasting our time. Maybe the wind is in the worse direction.

Josey Stay, Dad. Fish!

Father (*turning to* **Josey**) Be quiet and silent, you cretin, can't you? There are no fish if I say so.

Josey Dad, be gentle with me. I am very excited and eager to see a fish.

Father Christ, do you not hear me? Will you not back away? Will you not go some distance there? Would you block my path?

Josey Fish away, Dad, fish away.

Father I'd rather crush you. I'd rather put my hands each side of your soft brain and pancake it. Do you think I want you running up here with me like a collie, a foolish collie that won't herd sheep without biting them? What class of a shitty boy are you? Will you not give me peace?

Josey We were up this morning at four, before even the night was gone. It was only morning by courtesy. You gave me bran and beer to drink, and we tied the rod and the line to your bicycle, and went off down the lane to the road. We have walked and ridden, me on the crossbar, for two hours, and now it is nearly daylight outside the storm. All night I was awake in the loft with Mick, breathing under the close wood, hot and shaking. I was going to fish with my father in the morning and we are here now. You did not take Mick.

Father I will kill you here. I have killed sheep in their flocks and flocks, and chickens' necks in their thousands, and I have swiped at rats in the sheds, and cut them in two with the spade. I have crushed more spiders in my time than a bird has cracked snail-shells. Do you think it would be a great thing for me to crush you? You are small and weak-headed.

Josey Dad, I am old and weak-headed. My hair is grey as yours. You lay on the threshold of the house like a flounder, staring up at Mick as he leaned over you in astonishment. You looked at him with your fish's eyes, and your heart stopped budging in your chest. And you never took Mick to fish, and he often asked me why was that.

Father You were my favourite, Josey. You were like a daughter to me. You were a lovely faithful daughter, as good as a dog. You honoured me. You were too stupid to look at me the way Mick did. You were too doltish to question. You were the half of me I preferred, you'd no brain to mar you. I wish I had been born like you, without a real thought in my head. You were the best half of me, the half of me I killed in myself always. Mick was the most familiar section of me. He could see me through and through.

Light gathers and moves around the **Father.**

Josey (*hunched, quietly, speaking to the ground*) Fish away, Dad, fish away.

The bed, as before. The space to the extreme right has a bright hard sunlight. **Mick** *is standing extreme right, leaning into the fall of the light, hands in trouser pockets, in his Sunday best: clean shirt, checked, with green tie, good jacket, a newer fishing hat with a small feather, all his clothes a little tight for him. He says nothing for the moment, while the following lighting changes take place: the sunlight persists for some seconds, then gradually a cloud goes over, shadowing the space inch by inch. A wind gusts at* **Mick,** *the sunlight edges back, and a glittering light rain falls in the same direction as the light falls.* **Mick** *does not move out of it. He leans into the sun-shower.*

Mick (*in a quiet mumble, it is a line from the Marx Brothers' film*) Room Service? Room Service? (*After a moment.*) Send me up a room.

His head dips an inch, and he cries with open eyes, not caring in the rain. After some seconds he is able to stop crying.

I was eager for them all, and at the same time didn't care much for them. It was the way Collins looked, the way he stared about him like a tiger, that I admired. Not the politics. Or it was the politics. It was the politics, certainly, but I suspected it was always going to be the spirit of the times that I and my like would remain where we were and make do with that. In the rain and the cow's muck, and the companionship of a soft-headed brother. Whiskey with a glow, and the brother-warm bed. You can strive, you can talk hard in a bar at night, and you want it to mean something, you have a few ideas how things might go when the business is done. What to set up and what to avoid, who to allow and who to resist, who is the mean man in the town and who the generous helper, the man with no thought for himself, who would lead best, and make decisions that would spruce up the farms and the feeling of the farmers. So there wouldn't be a burden ever again, or any loss, or any misdemeanour. That we wouldn't be fodder for books again, that we wouldn't be called peasants in a rural district, and be slipped into the role of joker by the foreigners from the cities. That we wouldn't have to stand on the roadside and watch the cars go by with creatures in them from outer space, plastic and cushions and clothes, another Ireland altogether, people who would mock our talk, and not see us, not talk to us except by way of favour. That we could be men of our country was all my wish, that we might have a country that would nurture us, a spirit to get us up the road and out of the rain. How is it that after every change and adjustment I still stand here in the same rain on the same mud, with the same sun laughing at me? And there's the time I stood in a bar with Mick Collins and told him we had the same name, and he said I seemed a very sound man, and thanked me for my part in the business. I said I would burn anything for him, shoot anyone, if we might have a nation after, a nation I would be a citizen of, an honoured ordinary man. And the world would hear of us, and wish to be near us. I said I would do the worst thing for him, if I might always wear my Sunday clothes and drive in a decent fashion over the roads, and get the damp out of my bones and he put his hands on my back as he was leaving and said he needed more men like me. Then he went off to his wars and I went back to the card-game in the little room and never said a word about him to the others. I was moved beyond telling them, I was aflame from my toes up my legs, it was a real feeling. I was going to walk across the fields with my legs on fire and walk over everything that was beating me down and set it aflame: my father would smile on the hearth and laugh at me in a different way than the sun: he would honour me. Then I would go out with his spade and a bit of cement and build up everything again, and put the good man in a big house, and leave the mean man to himself. There was a lot to be done.

Now the good man I had my eye on is a man on his own in the neighbouring farm, with a bicycle for vehicle and a mossy house, and his sole adventure is the shopping trip to Bantry on a Tuesday. I was to make everything watertight for Collins, and be a decent man in my own district. I was never, myself, to stand carelessly in the rain again. I was to be a dry man with responsibilities.

The bed gone. Outside the house. Dull overcast light for the main part, now and then a sweep of sunlight passes from right to left. **Mick** *is sorting tools in a toolbox, humming. The sound of hooves walking on clattering stones is heard, at which* **Mick** *stands straight and watches.* **Josey** *comes on from the right, leading a 'horse'. Aspects of the horse are suggested by light.* **Josey** *responds to its movements: his hands go up and he admonishes the horse when it chucks its head. It is a big animal.* **Josey** *stops and pulls on the unseen rope.*

Josey Hup, hup.

He walks, and brings up the animal to where **Mick** *is.* **Mick** *backs away when the horse pushes its flank against him.* **Mick** *smooths the horse's nose and the horse pushes against his hand, and* **Mick** *laughs.*

Josey Stand now, Charlie, stand.

Mick Go back there. (*Pushing his flank.*) Go back.

Josey Is he to stand or go back?

Mick Hold him steady by the halter.

Josey Is he looking well to you?

Mick He looks fine.

Josey He does too, the creature.

Mick How's the grass up there?

Josey Not great at that. A bit sparse. He has more mud made under the rowanberries than a herd of bullocks.

Mick Poor old fellow, poor old fellow.

He strokes the horse's big neck and slaps it. These sounds, the patting, the horse shifting his hooves on the rocky ground, are heard. The horse snorts heavily.

Josey Oh, the man. Would we be as well to do his mane? It's very knotted.

Mick He's a lovely big girl.

Josey A big girl? This great gelding?

Mick What was the farrier's name, that used to come?

Josey Driscoll. The songwriter.

Mick Hold him now, and I'll pare him.

He bends down at the near hind, and tries to pull up the hoof, facing away from the animal, aiming to draw the leg up between his own legs.

Mick Come on.

Josey Raise it up, raise it up. Charlie knows you're only a tailor.

Mick *struggles with the leg, and gets it resting on his thigh. With a pliers from the box he pulls the 'nails' of the loose 'shoe' and prises the 'shoe' off and throws the pliers (as if with the shoes and nails) back in the box with a clatter. He takes the parer and cuts some of the 'hoof'.*

Mick Do you want to give me that new shoe? Give me a mouth of nails.

Josey *hands him a shoe and some nails from a pocket of his jacket, and* **Mick** *puts the nails in his mouth, five, that jut out.* **Mick** *fits the shoe against the pared 'surface' (his hand holds the shoe the necessary distance from his thighs) and pares some more. The horse forces his leg down and moves forward a bit, going sideways.*

Mick Hold up, can't you.

Josey He's a devil for that.

Mick He's a rogue. Come on up now, Charlie.

Mick *bends again and takes up the hoof and leg and puts the shoe against the 'hoof'. He takes a nail from his mouth and takes up the hammer and beats in the first nail, and does this with the other nails with a rhythmical tapping. The horse snorts loudly.*

Mick Keep him steady now, Josey. (*Throwing the hammer in the box, dipping for a file, filing off the hoof. The sound of this is heard.*)

Josey Steady now, stand.

Mick Rightyo. (*Dropping the 'hoof' and stepping away, throwing the file in the box, with the shoe and its nails at the same time.*) Is the lower gate hasped?

Josey Aye.

Mick We can let him be here then. He'll be safe enough.

Josey *takes off the invisible halter with some effort, because the horse holds his head high. The sound of the horse walking away calmly, and snorting again.*

Mick Fine so. The other feet are fine?

Josey Ah sure yes.

Mick Sound. Tea, so. He has slain me.

Outside. More overcast, darker with the threat of rain, slatey. **Josey** *is standing left of centre, more downstage than* **Mick***, who is standing idly.* **Josey** *is looking up at the sky, facing us.*

Mick (*singing vaguely and softly, suddenly*) Hoot en night en noot en night en noot en night en nyah.

Josey *shakes his head slowly at the sky.*

Mick (*suddenly again*) Hoot en night en noot en night en noot en nyah.

Josey (*suddenly, after a bit, looking up still*) It smells like vultures.

Mick (*turning away, walking upstage, light going*) Come on, Josey.

Josey *after a bit follows him. As they move upstage, curtain falls.*

Act Two

The kitchen. **Mick** *on his knees putting a match to the fire. The light increases slowly during the next few minutes of talk, finishing at the full glow of the fire. Noise of hard heavy rain falling outside.*

Mick That'll be it now for the whole of October, and November too maybe.

Josey (*right, in the shadows*) Cheese and bread I'm making.

Mick As long as you make tea I don't mind what I eat. I've no taste left much.

Josey I stood on the road this late evening and Brady talked to me. He said the boy in the top farm –

Mick What boy?

Josey Away up there where the waterfall is, and the mountain meadow – we were up there as lads. It is full of black pools. I remember it. There's a farm under the lot.

Mick Of course there is. (*Rising.*) You mean Jack Dillon's place.

Josey Well, he's dead.

Mick Jack?

Josey He died in the county hospital. He was in for a stomach complaint and got a pneumonia while he was there. Off he went.

Mick He was afraid of the hospital. He used to shovel stomach powders into himself. I saw as many as a score of empty tins in his parlour. (*Sitting on his stool, left.*) His mother was dead a long time.

Josey Brady said it was a sudden affair.

Mick He'd know.

Josey Will you go down to Killarney for the funeral?

Mick I won't.

Flash of lightning, illuminating the left window.

Josey They wouldn't be expecting you.

Mick Give me that bread, will you? He had no one.

Josey *comes to the fire, and hands him a saucer of sandwiches, and a cup.*

Mick Grub.

Thunder outside.

Josey I didn't see the flash.

Mick You were cutting cheese, man.

Josey Peeling it off, anyway. The wood will be soaked.

Mick It will be burned. I stacked it in. The turf's good though. We weren't cheated.

Josey Is that our turf?

Mick It's Carney's. I didn't dig a sod this year. My foot is banjaxed all summer.

Josey It's a poor thing when we burn someone else's turf. Did you pay money for it?

Mick I did not. He owed me many a favour. Don't you remember that great long week spent putting up his wire fencing?

Josey Was I with ye?

Mick (*laughing*) As far as I know.

Josey Well, there now.

Mick Sit, can't you?

Josey I'll call in the dog.

Mick (*quickly*) Don't start that.

Josey Is the father in?

Mick Don't start that either. I won't stand it. I'll have to go out.

Josey (*turning away to the shadows, right*) I suppose he's caught at the fair. Why did we bring no sheep to the fair this time?

Mick It's not fair day, is why. I have two ewes I want to sell on that day. I am sick of looking at them. There'll never be lambs in those ewes. They're only shadows of sheep. They're just grass-eaters.

Josey Would they stew?

Mick If you had a year spare to boil them.

Josey Well, so, I'd sell them quietly.

Mick Some of them half-wit farmers from Kenmare might go for them.

Josey Why not? They're grand sheep.

Mick Are you eating over there in the dark? The fire's warm now. (*After a bit.*) Bring your chair over here can't you, man dear.

Josey Where's that father at all? (*Coming over with his chair, and a cup.*)

Mick Did you eat?

Josey What's eating? I've no hunger. (*Looking into* **Mick**'s *cup.*) You have cinders splashed on it.

Mick I raised the ashes when I swept. You need fuelling, man.

Josey Eat yourself. Go on.

Mick I will. (**Josey** *sits.*) That's a terrible rain. We'll be stuck with it now for a month. We'll be like fish in here now for a month.

Josey The wood will be very wet.

Mick I stacked it, heart. (**Josey** *gets up.*) What's troubling you?

Josey I'm going to piss.

A bright green light, and yellow light, as if a hedgerow, appears in front of **Josey**. *He stands in the midst of this light. A young* **Girl** *with very thin poor hair and ill-dressed, rickety and frail and scrawny as a hen, approaches.* **Josey** *ducks back. The girl looks morose, off-putting, and sick.* **Josey** *holds out his arms at her and smiles. Rook noises. The* **Girl** *does nothing, does not look at him.* **Josey** *jumps at her and flattens her on the ground, noiselessly, and rolls off. The* **Girl** *gets up and walks on. Lighting returns to kitchen as before.*

Mick What happened to you?

Josey I tripped on the linoleum.

Mick (*getting up and helping him*) You poor old sod. Have you pulled anything?

Josey I've not pulled the hernia anyway. I must be all right. I don't feel anything.

Mick It's not good for an old man to fall. You'll have arthritis on the bumps for Christmas. (*Laughs.*)

Josey I'm a very clumsy sort of man, I expect.

Mick You're not. You're a dancer. A real dancer. Catch your breath.

Josey God bless me, I've pissed.

Mick You shocked yourself. You confused yourself.

Josey I hate that. All wet. (*He shakes his trousers a little.*) Tch, a poor excuse.

Mick Wear your Sunday.

Josey (*astonished*) On a Monday? Are you ill? I'll put on the old brown jobs.

Mick Josey, boy, you have more holes in them than a cloth. They're a walking disgrace.

Josey They're dry though. I'll have a rash on me if I linger now.

Mick Take them off, take them off, I'll get my other pair for you.

Josey Oh, that will be grand. I like those trews. They have a kind of shine to them.

Mick From sitting on my arse by the heat.

Josey *laughs with his head back, very strangely.*

Mick *standing at the dark rectangle of the left window, suggested by grey-blue light. The window is quite big, a front window of a circa 1910 farmhouse.* **Josey** *is sitting by the glow of the fire, sunk into the heat.*

Mick It is in spate, the river. It is a dangerous thing for Brady's cattle. Fools of people. (*After a bit, shaking his head.*) Jack Dillon's waterfall, a wonder after rain. It was full of salmon once, that big stream. Pig farmers! (*After a bit.*) You sold them in scores to the Commercial Hotel, formerly. (*After a bit.*) You wouldn't know what a flood would raise. I can't eat a salmon. Why would I?

Josey (*vaguely, low as if it is a formula*) He has left us in our place, that man.

Mick I wonder now, I wonder.

Josey (*low*) I never touched a woman in my born days. I'll sit inside this downpour forever.

Mick (*not looking back, but addressing* **Josey**) Do you want to start marrying someone? Where would you seat her? This farm would not divide. It is already a scrap.

Whinny of the horse outside, and a fall of light as he passes the window. His shape can be made out.

The big soft girl.

Josey But I never touched a girl, unless you count the lass I knocked down in the lane.

Mick If you don't knock them down, they won't lie down at all.

Josey You never did it. It makes a man strange to himself. It is more breaking bones in a sack to add them to pigfeed, than any other thing.

Mick If you don't knock them down, they won't lie down at all. The people in this valley are very silent. Just as well, sometimes. (*After a bit.*) The roads will be streaming. (*After a bit.*) The people in this valley are as far away from each other as old ships in a fog in an old sea-story. There's a fog of rain that keeps them apart. Only the fiddles kept any sort of company going. (*After a bit.*) TV aerials.

Josey If he ever had any thought of vengeance, he has it now certainly.

Mick He has. (*After a bit.*) Except we are like married people. We sleep in the same bed like the wed. It is like a marriage. (*After a bit.*) Did he plan that, I wonder, him who seemed to despise Mam's company while she breathed? When she was dead, he mourned her, tilled her plot like a little field, sowed it with a harvest of snowdrops. You'd think she had been a fine film star –

Josey Hail Freedonia!

Mick A woman in ermine, stepping along in black and white, with a glister of moonlight on a Californian bay, and a dead man sunk under the jetty. Is that what he aimed at for us, a little marriage for her sake? Didn't I plot and plan to go to New York, where the tailoring would have been a good profession, instead of jobbing down there in the town for forty years, making jackets for the lunatics in the asylum, such jackets that hitched their arms, making them swing, putting a true mark of madness on the poor men. I made madmen mad-looking in my time. (*After a bit.*) I sleep in his dip.

Josey But why vengeance on myself? I was his favourite.

Mick Josey, it was vengeance on me only.

Josey You think I can sit here like an old gaslamp in peace?

Mick No other peace would've suited your temperament, man.

Josey I'd like to tell you, I had high hopes once, sitting in the flea-pit of Killarney, of going west myself in a train, feeding the carriages into the engine, and arriving in due time. I had no other hope in life than to be a Marx brother, a worthy ambition I should think.

Mick It was. You should have had your chance, Josey, instead of being stuck here on a hill-farm with me.

Josey Aye.

Mick (*quietly*) That I might find the big scissors that would cut this farm in two. That I might eat my way through the sheep, and go to some glittery big city, with long cars in it.

Josey Aye, and injuns, and wagons, and those big open farms with grass waving on them for days.

Mick And drink at a distant bar, after work, and go home with a confident step, and put meat on the table in a brown parcel for my wife, who would be old now but pretty with make-up, like Mrs Molloy. To think that the girl I would have met, in some park or in some street, is now an old one like myself, and it was someone else she met and kissed, and was nervous talking to, and then grew stronger with. And all these years of seasons and floods, of greenery and streams and mud and whiskey nights, she has cleaned her American home, and looked out at the brisk sunlight without me.

Josey I always wanted one of them furcoats, the sort that makes the head look like a lost moon, Mick, and a pair of them shining socks. I'd look like a scarecrow in them, but I could be happy in such attire. I might walk the length of the towns, and print my footstep in concrete like Charlie Chaplin, laughing with a jerk at me in the cinema. Now how did he know I was there to see him, to give me that laugh?

Mick He gave it to us both.

Josey I was always very like that boy that roomed with Charlie Chaplin. I might have been the boy.

Mick You were the boy. You were always the boy. And you always wore a fur coat too, in effect.

Josey (*after a bit*) He foxed us for fillies, God's truth.

Rain as before. **Josey** *in the chair still.* **Mick** *is warming his hands and back at the fire near him. When he speaks he almost hisses.*

Mick Strange black hair, long red face, hard hands, good at shelling peas, soft lap enough, not a local woman. TB – Mam.

Josey Rightyo . . . Mam.

Mick Is that how you recall it?

Josey I don't recall anything about it at all.

Mick She kept hens there, in that very yard, such hens as few wouldn't want to own for themselves. She had three dresses, Mam, one black for deaths, one blue with white dots for wear, and a grey one for music. There were no bought clothes then, not up here.

Josey Was she fair?

Mick Listen to me. She was red-faced, black-haired. She couldn't speak a word of English or any other tongue.

Josey Was that the way?

Mick She kept her own counsel to the last degree. (*After a bit.*) Silent all her life, except for peculiar grunts. She waved her arms a deal. When she shelled peas, she used a tin dish for them, and had a flick in her wrist that sent each row of peas in hard, with a kind of pattern. She could do it with my head on her lap. I watched the sky, and ting, ting, ting, went the peas behind my ears. I could hear her smiling. You have to get on with things.

(*After a bit.*) Thirty years old. If I saw her on the road now she'd look like a child. She was a great beauty, I should imagine. (*After a bit.*) No. (*After a bit.*) She could walk of course, and listen. She could hear the rain begin to fall over Bantry, seven miles away. She'd have the sheets in off the bushes in a twinkle, you wouldn't know why. The rain would be along presently. That's a talent.

Josey rises, and goes to the smaller window on the right, where the old fiddle is.

She scolded us with her hand. She seemed to make a favourite of me, I think. I appreciated it. But she didn't scorn you, nor neglected to tend to you, Josey. You were a wild boy often. You could throw a fit quicker than a rook in a tree of rooks. You were often a very wild rook, boy.

Rook noises. **Josey** *comes back with the fiddle and its bow.*

Josey Listen to me now. I'll make it talk anyhow.

He plays the untuned strings, a scraping with the occasional note.

Mick (*in a gap in the playing*) Good. Lamentable but good. (*After a bit.*) Good man, Josey.

Stage darkens. Four figures dance slightly, with their backs to us from the right, in a line. They are wearing cloaks at the back. **Josey** *has his eyes closed in the murk. He plays on. The dancers turn briefly, with the same step in unison that* **Josey** *did earlier, splaying one hand, putting forward one foot. On this side they are wearing the costumes of chorus line dancers, glittery. They are large women. This happens briefly, then they turn their backs again, and dance off. Light as before.*

Mick (*after* **Josey** *stops*) I don't know what the hell the tune was, but it put me in mind of something. How she was always very mouselike when he played. A great big woman like that.

Josey I don't have the name of the tune.

Mick It was a great pity.

Josey I never had it.

Mick No, that she was dumb. She was the kind of person you wanted to apply to for answers on certain matters. She had an awful clever look to her often.

Josey I expect.

Josey *is now asleep on the chair.* **Mick** *is over to the right, where a smaller smudge of windowlight is, the dark glimmer of a small window on the weather side of the farmhouse, where the fiddle is kept. He holds the fiddle in his hands, looking at it.*

Mick If you can play this you can do a lot. It has strings like Charlie's tail, very wisps of music, a music that has died in my hands and Josey's. There were tunes in this fox-coloured thing that would . . . When our legs were spindles in the school trousers we danced to his tunes, like fools of lambs. What's this silent tune we dance to now, the rain's hammers?

Mick *stays quiet in the shadows. A patch of light shows the* **Mother** *in a blue and white dress, with a bowl and a few pods of peas. She is sitting downstage left. As she shells each pod deftly, she aims the peas into the bowl, where they rattle. She hums a tune silently, almost angrily. She gathers herself and gets up and carries the bowl and the empty pods over to the right, the light going with her as if a private atmosphere, to where* **Mick** *stood before in the rain.* **Mick** *is visible in shadow some way upstage of her. A further light beams down on her, falling from right to left. She holds out her arms slightly, pods in one hand, bowl in the other, and turns her face to the light, eyes closed, begins to smile, and holds herself there. After a while the light thickens, and rain falls lightly at a slant to her. She laughs lightly for a little, silently.* **Mother** *goes off right, previous lighting returns.* **Mick** *smooths the body of the fiddle, looks at the dust on his fingers.*

Mick There's varnish on her still, under the cake of mildew and paw-prints there's a shine on the old creature. You could play this and be young. Young and be still in your heart's kindness, young as a white potato in the drill, a new spud for the pot or the pit, for to give a man and his brother life. Now they kill

brothers in policemen's quarters, they bring them out into a yard
among the back buildings. I've heard this as clearly as a badly
bowed tune, as clear as an ill dream or a clatter of rain. They ask
the brothers in for questions, clean out their pockets and their
toothbrushes, brought in in expectation of a long night of asking
and telling, strip them down gently, picture them, and beat
them. The brothers are old enough, one belly a bit fat, sagging
under the ugly lights. They are beating the brothers under the
lamps, the older one, the heavy old one buckling, what distance
those legs have traipsed, buckling, at the belt of a whittled stick,
a stick to answer promptly. Buckling in the light, in a hard time,
to make you stop and think – 'Sweet life' you are thinking,
'Sweet life', everything of value is your brother, your tobaccos
and papers and talks, your dreams, your hope held up as a poor
cloth for protection and secrecy. So the old brother goes down to
the gravel ground, a thing to watch with a bloody look, his blood
in your eyes. The brother goes down, buried in his own messes,
and you return to the gates of the prison alone. Nothing, no
fiddle full of early days and boys' legs cavorting like goats, can
bring him back. I think then, thanks for my old sleeping brother,
unbeaten, as quiet as an owl in our house here on a hill above a
new flood. Let me stand between him and all harms, all human
harms, if no one better's to be found.

As before, but **Mick** *is now centrestage. The bright green and yellow bush
lights, as with* **Josey** *and the* **Girl** *before, form around him. The* **Girl**
approaches, not looking at **Mick**. **Mick** *steps into her path, and stoops
towards her. The* **Girl** *is staring, not seeing, at his chin, stalled.*

Mick Did you ever see a brown trout in a deep, muddy hole?
You did not. But he is there. (*Getting more and more severe.*) Did
you ever see a chick turn in his egg, in the liquid? You did not.
Did you ever see the bladder of a mare, as she stalls in the fields,
hindlegs splayed, and thrashes a pillar of piss on the grass? You
could not have.

Girl Out of my path and let me home.

Mick Did you ever admire the look of a white slug on a fresh young cabbage, plucked from the leaf and set down on the wooden draining board, did you ever come out in the morning and find the world of your farm stitched and corded with trails, snails' journeys that have no rhyme or reason? Did you never play foot-the-ball as a child and step on a snail, and hear the wet crunch, and curse yourself? Did you never see your father take up a tiny pup, and put its tail in his mouth, and bite it off, blood trailing down his chin?

Girl Out of my path and let me home.

Mick Did you ever rise to the bait of a corner-girl, get confused in a town by cries and accounts and askings, did you never feel the trouble of a girl as she walked in front of you, agitating her skirts, making her bottom stick? Did you not, indeed? Were you never mocked, giggled at and ruffled, did you never carry your shame into an alleyway, and cry for yourself, hugging your jacket? Did you never sweat in the summer dark, did you never lie in dirty sheets, gripping yourself like a lever you could use to drive out along ploughland, did you never hear a priesteen tell you that girls had no yen for anything, no moisture, no need, no cry, no thoughts? You did not. Did you never have to stop in the street crippled by your own blood, your poker jammed in your trouserleg, in such a manner as was plain to the every passer? You could not have. Did you never pray under soaking leaves, and wipe warm, white seeds in a cloth of jelly off your gansey? Did you never smell your own stinking perfumes, feel your body constrict in a queer mess, did you never ask the sky for a girl to hold your shoulders, stroke your forehead, say something to you you could store up for a hundred times? Did you never look in your pantry of sweet remarks and find it ever bare – bare in boyhood, barer in manhood, barest in first old age? You did not.

Girl Out of my path and let me home.

Mick Do you think we are not princes, Josey and me on the hill? Do you think he could not honour you? Do you think he would always knock you on the track? Do you think he has been taught anything? Do you not see the gentle cogs in him? Do you not hear his engine whirring gently? Do you not see a moon in each of his eyes, brown eyes without whites or pupils? Do you not see a creature that would care for you? He would walk over every townland telling farmers of you, if he only knew how to do it. Do you think all the talk he has heard in his school, in the roads, in the lanes, on the gates of farms, has anything to do with him? Do you not think it is just a crust, a dirt on him, that you could wipe off if you knew the trick of it, and discover under it the house of the cleanest snail? Do you not see that, if he was unsuitable, I would do, as much for you as himself, if you were generous, and could see me in this matter?

Girl Out of my path and let me home.

Then, in her own light, her face turned away from **Mick.**

His mother was a bad speaker. A rat stole her tongue. She was hard to work. She was a slave. She bore a tailor's goose, an idiot-man. The river is the better man, good for clothes, and for drowning. Here goes nothing. There were lights, there were lights to find me.

The same, **Girl** *gone. The rain has stopped.* **Josey** *is still asleep.* **Mick** *is standing where he was with the* **Girl.** *Now and then* **Josey** *whimpers in his sleep, like a dog.*

Mick (*to wake him*) Josey.

Josey *whimpers again.*

Mick (*walking to the stool*) Josey. You sound like Shep.

The **Father** *comes on from the left, stands between them in front of the fire.*

Father (*looking at* **Josey**) The old cretin. What use is he to you?

Mick (*not looking at* **Father** *but at* **Josey**) He is every use to me. He is the thing I know.

Father (*putting out his left hand and taking a toothbrush from* **Mick**'s *breast pocket*) What do you carry this for?

Mick In case someone might think us uncivilised.

Father And do you use the item much?

Mick (*thinking, then after a bit*) A great deal.

Josey (*waking, at which* **Father** *goes off left*) Warm. My heavens on earth.

Mick What is it?

Josey I dreamt something.

Mick You'll toss all night in the bed, sleeping down here like that.

Josey Old men may dream.

Mick What class of a dream was it?

Josey I have not the least remembrance of it. It was water though. There were lamps. Lamps of a pony-and-trap, not a car. The old high lamps, brass lamps, stuck up on poles that pony-and-traps had. If there was ever a beautiful contraption in this valley, it was a pony-and-trap. (*He wipes his face in his hands.*) Well.

Mick It's a dark night. Do you want to go up?

To the left, a circle of light around the **Mother**, *where she was sitting before, kneading the clay around the roots of a geranium in a clay pot.* **Mick** *steps back towards her light, and settles on the ground a little away from her, watching what she is doing.*

Mick Mam.

The **Mother** *looks up briefly.*

Mick How's Mam?

The **Mother** *nods at him, pressing the clay still.*

Mick There's a very strange trick in the town now.

She looks at him.

Mick No, there is, there is. I'll tell you. I was down there after school. A few of the lads were talking about the new contraption they've set up for the sake of Moran's Meeting Rooms. So I went in myself for the mischief. It was a most unusual thing. It's like a beer mug with a lid, but it's big and white, and under the lid there's a seat for your backside.

The **Mother** *stops kneading and raises her fist to him, smiling.*

Mick Well, there is. I can't help that.

The **Mother** *encourages him with her forehead.*

A big thing enough. I was marvelling at it. It was filled with water, you'd think it was for drinking out of, or washing your paws, the water was so clean.

Mother *laughs silently.*

You see, Mam, you're to regard this contraption as a sort of quiet spot, like a clay pit.

Mother *looks at flowerpot, nods.*

It was a marvel, the clearness of the water, and what they expected you to do in it. I wouldn't have pissed in it for the world.

Mother *shushes him briefly, laughs.*

Mick *walks back to where he was, while* **Mother** *goes off left. Previous lighting.*

Josey Give us a time here still with ourselves. We've not much on, have we? Will you bury the spuds tomorrow?

Mick They're in.

Josey Fair dues.

Mick I don't know. I went through the leg of the dog doing it.

Josey Where? Over by the whitethorn?

Mick You shouldn't bury animals in good earth. You'd no marker nor other stone to tell me. You put him in there because the soil was soft from last year's pit. It was less work for you. But a potato pit is not a grave, man.

Josey He'll salt the spuds for us.

Mick I filled him in again and dug afresh.

Josey Fair dues. (*He strokes back his hair.*) I was tired and dry earlier.

Mick Jesus Christ.

Josey How, Jesus Christ? A lovely man he was, with a skirt.

Mick I'm stymied. I'm like a bullock stuck in a bog. I feel that if I move again, I'll never be contented.

Josey What do you mean? On the floor there, stymied, do you mean?

Mick Stymied.

Josey You were always stymied, weren't you? Stymied was your tune.

Mick Aye. There's no sense in me.

Josey There's only very little. You are almost a halfwit.

Mick The pot and the kettle.

Josey Are you asleep? You have the room troubled.

Mick I should have gone down to the town tonight. I'm not myself.

Josey Well, you should have suited yourself. I was asleep completely. I might have slept till you came home. It's always home here.

Mick I'll go out and walk. I'll go up to the top field a little way and look down on our roof. That helps me. I am shivering like a lamb. I must have been born in the snow.

Josey Go on out. Talk to the horse for a minute. Don't fall over.

Mick I'll go out for a little while. The starlight will do me good. I'll look at the boulders going up the back of the farm, or talk to the horse. I'll be able to see the old dun if there's a moon, or imagine it.

Josey It will be muddy after the rain. Don't fall on a loose bit of ground.

Mick If everything is dripping, I'll be content again. It is a lovely sound, the dripping bushes.

Call of stranded cattle below.

Josey Sheep on a hill are best, poorer but best.

Mick That must be some water now, in the channel.

Josey Go out and see it.

Outside. Dark, rush of river below. A patch of daylight grows on the threshold, showing the heap of the **Father**, *lying on his side, his face turned upwards.* **Mick** *leans into the circle of daylight, bending over the figure.*

Father (*softly*) What's this putty in me?

Mick How will I help you?

Father When I breathe, I can feel putty moving in me, with hardship.

Mick Will I pillow some part of you?

Father It is an uncomfortable thing, being full of hard putty.

Mick Will I warm it in my fingers?

Father Go away out from me, I am not used to you.

Mick Should I fetch something? Some other person?

Father Pray for me.

Mick (*unhappily*) What did you say?

Father I said, pray for me, are you hard of hearing?

Mick Our father who art in Heaven, let me talk to this man before it is impossible. Amen.

Father That is a bad, ill-sounding prayer.

Mick It is my prayer.

Father I suppose you'd like to stamp on me?

Mick That isn't what I want.

Father Ah, go away with yourself somewhere, and let me lie.

Mick (*trying again*) Father most wayward, pray for –

Father Pray for me properly, you fool!

Mick Accept this most beautiful, most wayward father among the other fathers.

Father *closes his eyes.*

Old fisher, goodbye.

Josey, *alone in the kitchen. He stands centrestage, facing the 'door'. When he talks, he talks conversationally, but with stilted gestures.*

Josey You might miss the travelling forge, Driscoll's, the songwriter, but there's no horses left for it. Charlie's the last man, the rare boy. You won't get a farrier to come up here now. There was a horse on every farm, sometimes two for a plough. Charlie is the last man. It will be a queer drop of water in the waterfall, I have seen that. I have seen that waterfall. There's a

thing about a flood that's rarely said – it is greedy for the fields.
It is a bull for them. You can't prevent it. Mick can not eat a
salmon! He could not touch one. There are none now, there are
none. The pigs ate them. The slurry, you know. You would want
to bring the cows up here when they call. They wish it. Once a
year in the flood they wish it heartily, to come up here with the
two dark men. (*Laughing.*) We will hold Charlie to the house the
winter, we will nurture him. We will bolster him, like our
bolster, on the bed above. Mick sleeps in his dip! She left none.
We could not have bolstered her. She died in blood, like a sheep,
she was a stick, a small stick. He was ever a pleasing horse! Even
from the furthest field he will come when I shout for him, he
wouldn't budge for a foreigner. He has no interest in sugar. Do
you want sugar in that, Mick? Don't poison it, he says!
(*Laughing.*) He is a wise old horse, but very old. Let him stick by
the house, certainly. He can pull the cart still, he enjoys himself
in the shafts. I saw the loose shoe when he brought up the wood,
I spotted it. (*Laughs.*) I can see, I can see. I saw that. He has
plenty of go in him still. But he's troubled by age. Princelike.
Holy. The very best. Isn't he? Brady's mare foaled him. Best.
God now. He has pulled, he has pulled a host of loads, turfloads,
timberloads, big sacks of grain and feed, bundles of firesticks like
farmers in coats. He is too old. We must guard him. The friend.

*He goes off left, the stage is empty. The length of the downstage section
begins to light more brightly, putting the upstage region generally in
shadow. The* **Mother** *comes on from the left with a bowl of henseed.
Clucking noises off. As she walks she flings the seed, but silently. When the
'hens', suggested by red brushstrokes of light, rush in, she seems to want to
drive them back with stamps of her right foot. She is wearing a black
dress. The seed that she casts is pierced and lit by sunlight, in beams from
low upstage. When she reaches centrestage,* **Josey** *comes on after her. He
is holding a dead rat by the tail.*

Josey (*holding himself in*) Mam, Mam.

The **Mother** *glances back and then goes on casting the seed, the sunlight
washing it till it falls.*

Josey Mam!

She turns properly and looks at him, and he raises up the rat for her inspection. She steps back a pace, and mimes for him to throw the rat away downstage. **Josey** *looks at her blankly. She mimes again. He flings the rat away into the dark of the stage. She sweeps forward and places her palm on his cheek softly enough, but with almost a blow, straightens his jacket, pushes him away by the shoulder gently, turns and walks off right, casting the seed. This time no light falls through it.* **Josey** *looks after her. He walks a little way after her. At centrestage he lies on the ground, curls somewhat, sleeps. Darkness for a space. Light of the kitchen fire returns, and when it does,* **Josey** *is still on the ground, but his feet are facing us, his legs and arms spread as if he is fastened at the ankles and wrists. As he says the first word, the room darkens and a clear yellow light falls on him.*

Josey (*quickly*) Mick!

He pulls on his invisible bonds.

Mick!

His head goes back and he rests. He jerks suddenly at the bonds, straining his face up to look in front and to each side of him.

Ghost of God! Mick!

The **Girl** *comes on, as odd and dirty as before. She walks on her knees.*

What is it?

She does not answer. She stops near him.

Where have you me? Am I far? Who has me tied?

Girl Did you ever put a buttercup under your chin and see the yellow?

Josey What has me tied up? Are you going to sell me? Is it fair day now?

Girl Yellow, yellow. A bad colour all told.

Josey Would you loosen me? I would pray for you if you could. I've no money.

Girl Did you ever notice how much improved the countryside is in a good summer – how the place looks very much another place? And gives you different hopes.

Josey Mick has the money, you see. I don't even see my pension. The post office gives it to him. Of course it is an ideal arrangement. I would lose it on the road back.

Girl It is very difficult though to understand the most of it. How you are to have hope, and then no hope, for the rest of the stint.

Josey Loosen me, please. I have a great crick in my neck from this.

Girl Rain falling on the mass – that's what I thought. We are all here, all of us, the sinners and the saints and the mixtures, inside the wooden church, and the rain is falling on us. On the mass.

Josey Can't you hear me? I was asking you many questions. Already you have answered none of them.

Girl We huddle in the porch. The whole townland almost in the one porch. Not much of a place if we are all there is to it. We've bred no one of any repute that I know of. It is not a world.

Josey Where am I here?

The **Girl** *turns on her knees and starts back.*

Wait now, wait now.

The **Girl** *stops.*

Girl (*not looking back*) Yellow, yellow. Bitter, bitter.

Josey That's a nice song.

Girl *starts to go again, and goes off.*

Josey Wait! What has me here? (*Quietly to himself.*) Tell me what keeps me.

Outside, noise of dripping and the rush of the swollen river below. There is a clear, dark, rinsed light, with high darkblue clouds crossing an otherwise lustrous night sky. The larger kitchen window is a rectangle of brighter light, illuminated by the fire inside. **Mick** *stands with his back to us, arms at his sides, staring at the house, silent. The figure of the horse goes slowly, quietly, head down, from left to right, passing some way in front of* **Mick**'s *back. After a time,* **Josey** *comes into the area of the 'door'. He looks at* **Mick**, *pauses on the threshold. He comes forward, places a hand on* **Mick**'s *shoulder, and brings him in.*

Inside the kitchen. The stairs are again visible on the right. **Mick** *and* **Josey** *stand a few feet inside the 'door'. The fire is low.*

Mick (*needing help*) Josey.

Josey Christ in His Heaven.

Mick What, Josey?

Josey Mick, I dreamed I was a girl. I fell asleep on the floor.

Mick What were you like?

Josey I was miserable.

Mick Much the same then.

Josey Oh, but I was very miserable, I wanted to go in the river quick.

Mick Dreaming. You'll have strange pains from the damp in that floor.

Josey I didn't want to be miserable. I was making a great effort. I was like a slave. (*Crying.*) I know nothing. I am a cretin.

Mick Do you know this fire? (**Josey** *nods.*) You're my brother. If you were ever a cretin I was one too. You were dreaming.

Josey *goes a few steps up the stairs.* **Mick** *is behind him, still on the floor.*

Mick There will be more rain. Of course there will be. (*Laughing.*) We're surrounded. The Indians. You never see them, they shoot from behind boulders. It is very much as they say. I think I'm done for. I don't think I can wait for those cavalry horses. (*Touching* **Josey***'s knee at the back.*) You hold out without me. You take my bullets. Don't waste your water on me. Don't let the Indians creep up on you. Keep your eyes peeled, Josey. Take my bullets. (*Taking his hand back, talking to no one.*) Is there no sign of them bloody horses?

They remain like that for a moment.

Josey There is. There is every sign.

Curtain.